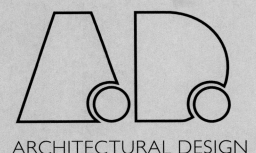

ARCHITECTURAL DESIGN

EDITORIAL OFFICES:
42 LEINSTER GARDENS, LONDON W2 3AN
TEL: 071-402 2141 FAX: 071-723 9540

EDITOR: Maggie Toy
EDITORIAL TEAM: Iona Spens,
Katherine MacInnes, Stephen Watt
ART EDITOR: Andrea Bettella
CHIEF DESIGNER: Mario Bettella
DESIGNER: Toby Norman

CONSULTANTS: Catherine Cooke, Terry
Farrell, Kenneth Frampton, Charles Jencks,
Heinrich Klotz, Leon Krier, Robert Maxwell,
Demetri Porphyrios, Kenneth Powell, Colin
Rowe, Derek Walker

SUBSCRIPTION OFFICES:
UK: VCH PUBLISHERS (UK) LTD
8 WELLINGTON COURT, WELLINGTON STREET
CAMBRIDGE CB1 1HZ
TEL: (0223) 321111 FAX: (0223) 313321

USA AND CANADA: VCH PUBLISHERS INC
303 NW 12TH AVENUE DEERFIELD BEACH,
FLORIDA 33442-1788 USA
TEL: (305) 428-5566 / (800) 367-8249
FAX: (305) 428-8201

ALL OTHER COUNTRIES:
VCH VERLAGSGESELLSCHAFT MBH
BOSCHSTRASSE 12, POSTFACH 101161
69451 WEINHEIM
FEDERAL REPUBLIC OF GERMANY
TEL: 06201 606 148 FAX: 06201 606 184

CONTENTS

Junga Toda *Temple of Laughter* Osaka, Japan

Imre Makovecz, Visegrád Camp, Hungary

Richard Rogers, Pumping Station, Royal Victoria Dock, London

BATTLE & McCARTHY
MULTI-SOURCE SYNTHESIS
Atomic Architecture

We presently process a variety of materials, cut them up into shapes and then fix them together to create the built environment for our particular needs. The majority of design resources are directed into trying to solve the technical problems brought about by the bringing together of different building components, whether they be structural, finishes, or service equipment of varying magnitude.

However, the advancement of material science is revealing a new construction process initiated at atomic level. Instead of cutting and stitching a patchwork of structural and non structural elements together in the hope that they will work in harmony, the atomic revolution will provide us with the means of creating building enclosures by the means of manipulating the molecular matrix and the atomic ingredients to the required structural and environmental specification, thus designing out the problem of building component interfaces. For example, using chemistry one will be able to orchestrate molecular geometry, transforming the material's strength and stiffness towards transparency without interruption. One can also even visualise the possibility of restructuring the very earth which bears the building to provide the necessary stiffness without the need for pouring thousands of tons of concrete into the ground in the form of foundations.

Molecular research into material performance is being approached by all building material and systems suppliers. In particular, the plastics industry and institutions including ICI and Cranfield University are investing huge resources into polymer research and development including being able to construct industrial components from small molecules without the necessity of melting and casting. The cloning of such a process will herald a new technical revolution in mass production of recycled atoms and molecular matrices.

This article focuses upon plastics technology. It examines the combination of carbon and hydrogen atoms and how they may be arranged in a variety of different geometrical configurations to create a range of different structural and environmental properties. It first briefly summarises the scope of plastics architecture and then describes in more detail the atomic structure of carbon and hydrogen which are the chemical ingredients of most plastics. It is completed with a brief insight into how polymer atomic science may construct strength, stiffness, transparency and insulation from different arrangements of carbon and hydrogen atoms.

Plastic Architecture

The architectural characteristics of plastics are more commonly associated with their manufacturing processes than with the properties of molecular configuration of the material. There are four main types of manufacture:
– injection moulded elements   – spouts
– cast/extruded elements   – pipes
– woven fibres   – tents
– reinforced resins   – yachts

There are over 10,000 different types of plastics which may be soft, tough, hard, brittle, transparent, opaque, combustible, self-extinguishing or incombustible and insulative or conductive. Plastics are organic materials based on carbon and hydrogen atoms. They are polymers, consisting of relatively simple repeating units combined into very large chains. They are called plastics because at some stage they are plastic; that is they can be formed into desired shapes in the liquid state, often by pressure and heat.

Our construction industry has evolved from the stone age into the iron age and now is a leading consumer into the plastics age. Presently, the world production of plastics outstrips production of steel and aluminium together and is expected to nearly double in the next twenty years. Our industry is the second major consumer of plastics after the packaging industry, and it is used with applications ranging from drain pipes to resin coated fabric roofs enclosing our stadia.

Molecular Structure of Plastics

The understanding of the molecular structure of common plastics starts with the carbon and hydrogen atoms and then follows with an examination of the different arrangements the carbon and hydrogen atoms may take up to become 'plastic' molecules.

Carbon atoms

The carbon atom is not solid. It consists of a

OPPOSITE: How atoms react with themselves or other atoms to create molecules of totally different characteristics is under investigation throughout the world; FROM ABOVE: A 1900 Thatcher using a leggatt to beat the thatch firmly into position; 19th-century molecular model of Mono-chloromethane; JJ Thomson (1856-1940) intended to be a railway engineer, but instead became a brilliant physicist. He discovered the atomic structure of atoms by passing cathode rays between high voltage terminals in a glass filled with low pressure gas

nucleus around which electrons orbit. If the atom was the size of Wembley Stadium the nucleus would be smaller than a tennis ball. The nucleus consists of protons and neutrons which are about 10^{-15} m across and have a mass of 1.7 x 10^{-27} kg. The electrons which orbit the nucleus are about one 2000th of the mass of a proton. The electrons are held in orbit by an electrical force similar to that of the static force one experiences when one combs one's dry hair. Carbon atoms are living atmospheres of energy, mostly empty space dotted with particles.

If the force between the atomic particles is broken, huge amounts of energy are released. A process more commonly associated with nuclear explosions and nuclear reactors. The width of a razor blade is over one billion atoms wide. However atoms can be visualised. Some of the best images have been generated by scanning the electrical variations related to the positions of the atoms with a scanning tunnel microscope. By recording these variations, the position of atoms may be determined.

Hydrogen atom
The hydrogen atom is much smaller than the carbon atom as it only consists of a single proton and an electron in orbit. Hydrogen is the smallest atom on earth.

Plastic Molecule
When two or more atoms come into contact, they may have no effect or they may react to form a new molecule. This is a chemical reaction. The carbon atom requires four additional electrons in its outer orbit to become stable. The hydrogen atom requires one more electron in its single orbit to become stable. Atoms are able to share electrons with other atoms to become stable, for example a single carbon atom may share four electrons with four neighbouring carbon atoms in a number of configurations:
- Tetrahedron   – Diamond
- Plane   – Graphite
- Sphere   – Buckminsterfullerene
Two hydrogen atoms may share electrons to form ordinary hydrogen gas, annotated as H_2.

In addition, the carbon atom may share the electrons with four hydrogen atoms creating CH_4 methane gas. However, adjacent carbon atoms can share electrons as well as sharing electrons with hydrogen atoms, creating C_2H_4 or ethylene.

Ethylene is the start of the carbon-hydrogen chain. Ethylene molecules may be activated to form a much longer chain. The chain starts as a monomer, then a dimmer, then a trimmer and so on to become chains of hundreds containing thousands of carbon and hydrogen atoms commonly known as polymers.

A chain based on ethylene C_2H_4 is called polyethylene, a well-known plastic, providing for example vapour barrier films and water pipes.

Atomic Structural and Environmental Engineering

Atomic structural and environmental engineering in architecture is concerned with maximising the use of atoms in configurations for the physical and environmental benefit of the user. Building structures require four fundamental performances including: support, light control, thermal control and ventilation.

There are perhaps fifty different types of atoms which may be orchestrated into geometries which fulfil each or a combination of the above needs. However, this article limits the discussion to the design developments of the carbon and hydrogen atoms only, as a simple means of demonstrating how one may design and manipulate the atomic structure for particular structural and environmental requirements, a process now known as Nano Technology.

Nano Techology
Scientists are daily creating new material properties by changing the atomic or molecular configuration. There are over a ninety different types of atoms and there is an infinite number of possible arrangements from which molecules may be formed. This indeed means that any desired mechanical or environmental property may be acquired upon demand. In fact, the scientists who place atoms on top of atoms in a similar manner to carrying and laying bricks on a building site call their operation architecture.

For example, carbon atoms may be rearranged from their weaker graphite formation into the strong diamond formation by pressurising the graphite layers together until they interlock to form the diamond tetrahedron geometry. In 1990, the Buckminster Fuller geodesic dome principle was reconstructed in carbon atoms, creating a single 'Buckminsterfullerene' molecular ball of 60 carbon atoms which forms an ideal lubricant.

Atomic architects are making huge strides in the creation of new molecules which have never existed before. Computers are used, very much in the way we simulate building form, to help the atomic designer to test various atomic arrangements before proceeding with construction. Construction may consist of exerting pressures or may be more sophisticated by using construction tools such as processors which harvest particular atoms for treatment. These processors themselves consist of 'constructed' synthetic molecules. Beyond building matter the 'atomic designers' are developing synthetic drugs which are designed to seek out and destroy diseases as well as replacing damaged organisms.

FROM ABOVE: Atoms are mostly empty space with tiny sub-atomic particles suspended in a cloud of energy. Charged with static electrical effects, like the electrical atomosphere in a thunder storm; scanning tunnelling microscope image which shows a single layer of carbon atoms in the form of graphite; OPPOSITE, FROM ABOVE L TO R: Bird's eye view of Hampton Court by Leonard Knyss in the early 18th century; newly created market such as windsurfing generates opportunities which can trigger research, just as a new product of the plastic age can create a new market; molecules are made with atoms. They become bonded together like human links on a free fall; atomic engineers use computer programs to construct molecules. The atoms are colour coded and positioned. Their positions can be modified and new atoms or groups of atoms can be added. The computer stores information about the forces between these atoms

Atomic Architecture

Fundamental structural and environmental performance requirements may be created through the selection of suitable atoms arranged in an appropriate manner.

Atomic construction

There are four fundamental structural/environmental material properties required:-
– strength
– stiffness
– insulation
– transparency

The following section describes how each of these properties may be achieved by rearranging the carbon and hydrogen atomic framework.

Strength

Unbranched carbon-hydrogen chains are denser and stronger than the more 'jumbled' configuration of branched chains, thus like pruning a rose tree the configuration may be pruned to become more linear. Cross-linking of the chains also increases the strength. The cross-linking of chains transforms a collection of individual atomic chains to a single solid molecule which is the basis of setting resins used in GRP boat construction.

The strength of polyethylenes may be transformed by replacing the hydrogen atom with another. If the hydrogen atoms are replaced with Fluorine for example, it then becomes a polymer known as POLYTETRAFLUORO-ETHYLENE, more commonly known as PTFE which is the resin used for most high strength tensile fabric roofs.

Stiffness

Stiffness is the ratio of the force of deformation. In polyethylene the carbon to carbon is stronger than carbon to hydrogen bond. Thus eliminating a pair of hydrogen atoms and doubling up the carbon to carbon bond of adjacent carbon atoms will increase the stiffness. Stiffness of the material may also be increased by 'straightening up' the molecular chain from a jumble to a more rational linear form.

If a cubic molecular structure is generated (as for rubber) the molecules may be elongated, and with the necessary applied energy, such as heat, the atoms will return to their original atomic configuration. These atomic frames are more commonly known as shape memory materials. If you heat an elastic band under tension for example, it will become shorter.

In the aerospace industry, vast resources are being invested into the research associated with the deformation and re-establishment of carbon-hydrogen geometry, to eliminate inflight thermal deformation of the plastic structural components of the wings and fuselage.

The deformation is counteracted by the atoms repeatedly returning to their original position. If such principles were developed for building components, one could imagine infinite stiffness for very little material, creating a new age in elegant structural design.

Insulation

As the temperature of a material rises, the atoms vibrate. The closer the atoms are to each other, the quicker the heat is transmitted. In gases for example, the atoms/molecules are further apart. This is why practical insulating materials are those that can successfully contain gas volumes above 90%. This may be achieved by raising the temperature of a polymer above the melting point where the inter-molecular forces holding the long chain molecules are broken down. Also the intermolecular forces that maintain a rigid linear configuration break down and the molecules coil up with each other in a manner analogous with boiling spaghetti on cooling. If on cooling, the atomic designer was able to maintain a vacuum between molecular chains, one would be able to generate super insulating properties, far in excess of what is presently available, ie a material as thin as this paper having insulative properties equivalent to over a foot of concrete.

Transparency

If the wavelength of light is able to pass through the molecular configuration, the material is known as transparent.

To ensure the polymer is transparent, the atomic designer needs to disrupt the packing efficiency of the polymer chains by rearranging the carbon-hydrogen molecular configuration to allow the free passage of light rays.

Conclusion

Thus provided with the knowledge and the 3D computer modelling facilities already available in most architectural and engineering offices, an architect too may proceed to generate a new understanding of materials at an atomic level with which we have all become so familiar.

Imagine designing an atomic structure, for example, which absorbed water molecules from a humid atmosphere and transmits them to the outside to be evaporated by solar radiation. Such a roofing and cladding material would provide humidity control for large public spaces in the tropics, thus avoiding the huge energy demand being sought by air conditioned airport terminals in the Far-East.

It is strange to think that if one replaced the carbon atom with a silicon atom and pairs of hydrogen atoms with oxygen, one would create from the common polythene chain the molecular basis for glass. Atomic architecture is more to

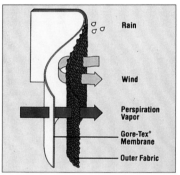

FROM ABOVE: In 1953 James Watson and Francis Crick made the DNA model. It comprises a large number of repeated elements with aluminium plates representing the four different bases; gortex material allows for the passage of air molecules but restrains water molecules

do with experiencing the mystery of 'atomic space planning' than solving the technical problems generated by the interaction of inappropriate materials. It may not be in our life time, although many scientists believe it will be when architects and engineers may design and construct a building from common atoms such as carbon, hydrogen, oxygen, silica, calcium and iron. In the future, the design team will be able to create the environmental space from a coherent arrangement of atoms which provide the necessary passive and active interaction with gravity, air movement and radiation for the least amount of atoms. These building materials may even be self-repairing. The high technology, not of the future but of the present.

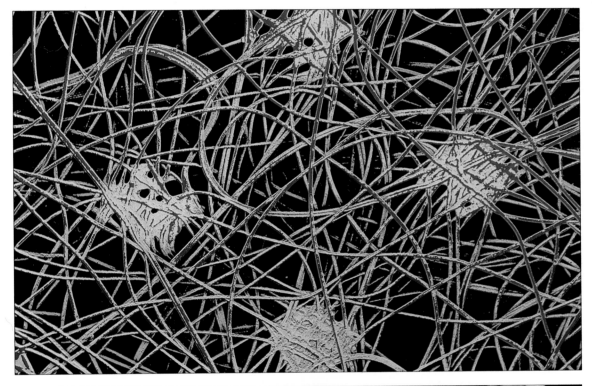

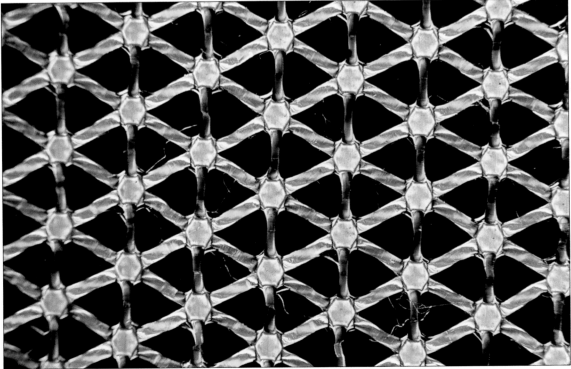

FROM ABOVE: False colour scanning electron micrograph (SEM) of the detailed structure of polypropylene (or polypropene) filaments. The filaments of this non-woven textile fabric are anchored by heat bonding. RE Litchfield; polarised light micrograph of a section of a biaxially oriented, stretched, high-density polythene net. This fabric is machined from man-made polythene fibres. The colours in the fibres appear in polarised light and correspond to residual stresses in the plastic fibres. Dr Harold Rose.

THE PERCEPTION OF SEEING
OBJECT OF DESIRE
Jayesh Sidpara

Architecture is understood as a kind of object to be looked at, inhabited by the viewer who is detached from it, inhabited precisely by being looked at, whether it be by the user, visitor, critic, or reader of architectural publications.

This general model of visuality still dominates current critical and theoretical discourse. The assumption about visuality and architecture which are written with the construction of theory remains unexplained and usually returns to tacitly organise theoretical work.

This visuality inscribed within architectural discourse not only produces the architectural *object as* such but cannot be separated simply from it: vision cannot be separated from the construction of space which in turn cannot be separated from the construction of gender upon which sexuality is place, usually violently

Leon Battista Alberti stated in *On the Art of Building in Ten Books* that 'the building is very much like an animal', using the example of men who choose their wives on the basis of the *shape of their bodies*. The beautiful body, whether it be building or a woman, is 'regulated' in a way that immediately *arouses, provokes,* and *excites* the mind. It is mans 'nature to desire the best and cling to it with pleasure'.

The arousal comes from the order that controls the sensuous surface. The sense of *her* dignity is *his* law, the beauty he desires is his own – his visual pleasure. Between the viewer and the subject there has to be distance. The phenomenon of seeing cannot keep or hold, though it may presume, intrude, trespass, distort, exploit, and the farthest of metaphor, violate.

Rooms with a View

Architecture is not simply a platform that accommodates the viewing subject. It is a viewing mechanism that produces the subject, it precedes and *frames* its occupants. Thus showing that the perception of space is not what space is but one of its representations, in this sense built space has no more authority than drawings, photographs, or descriptions.

For Adolf Loos architecture was also a form of covering, but it was not the walls that were covered. The spaces of Loos interiors cover the occupants as clothes cover the body – each

occasion having the appropriate 'fit'. All the architecture of Loos can be explained as the envelope of a body; from Lina Loos' bedroom, seen as a bag of fur and clothes, to Josephine Baker's swimming pool, a transparent bowl of water. The interiors always contain a warm bag in which to wrap oneself. It is *an architecture of pleasure.* This employed notion is similar to that of the *striptease act,* in that a woman is de-sexualised at the very instant she is stripped naked. It may be said that we are therefore dealing with a spectacle based on fear, as if eroticism travels no further then a kind of pleasing terror, whose ritual signs have only to be announced evoking instantly the idea of sex and its magical connotation. It is only in the removal of clothing that makes voyeurs of the public. Thus in a striptease a whole series of coverings are placed upon the theatrical stage and upon the body of the woman as she pretends to shed it bare. The elements of demystifying the spectacle through the decor, the props and the stereotypical clothing – the fans, the feathers, the gloves, the fishnet stockings, in short the whole spectrum of adornment associated with fetishism that constantly returns to the living body to the category of luxurious objects which surround women with mysterious decor.

The Josephine Baker House, by Adolf Loos, Paris 1928, is an extremely crude example of how the exhibit, Josephine Baker (note she no longer represents a living person) is transposed as a fetishistic object to stir the audience's curiosity. The house was designed to contain a large top-lit, double height swimming pool, with entry from the second floor The first floor walls surrounding the pool are realised by wide windows visible from the outside. Thick transparent glazing is let into the side of the pool to make it possible to *watch* the swimming and diving within its crystal clear water, flooded by light from above, *an underwater revue bar.*

The house has a secret locked away. This motif suggests a metaphoric representation of myths associated with the female body, and extends the image of concealment, the container, the secrecy. . . The inhabitant, Baker, has been made the sole item and the visitor, the guest, is the onlooking subject. The most intimate space, the swimming pool, has been positioned as the focal point of the visitor's view.

Allen Jones Desire me, *1968, USA*

The pleasurable experience gained in the house is by *looking*. However, between the glazing and water the body is made inaccessible, *look but don't touch. . .* The fetishization of the exterior is bought into the interior. From the window, peepholes, the viewers can fetishize Baker's body as a surface adhering to the windows, and like the body, the house is all surface, a screen with no interior. Munz attempted to analyse the characteristics of the project but ended by writing that ' *they look strange and exotic'* .It is quite odd that a writer with such rich architectural background is left unsure as to whether he is referring to the model of the house or to Miss Baker herself. He seems quite unable to either separate himself from the project or to enter it.

This analogy runs parallel to the sex shows widely accessible throughout the world. Again, the female being used more excessively and discriminately in our *visual culture*. Like the vibrant exterior of the Baker house brightly coloured neon lights invite customers to satisfy their curiosity to what is behind the door. The door can trigger off many emotions to enhance the sense of eagerness, it represents the crossover from another space, emitting the element of surprise and danger. Once inside, a *personalised viewing theatre is* created. Anonymity is secured by the arrangement and sizes of each theatre box. No more than one person at a time may enter, permitting various acts of voyeurism to be realised and fulfilled.

A mental game is produced teasing the customers voyeuristic eagerness. As one enters through the doors, A, the only internal object viewed is that of the counter where the guardian of the door, the salesman, sits reflecting the sense of excitement lurking ahead of them. To heighten the curiosity either a double partition, as in X, or another door, as in Y, is placed. By this time the voyeur has overcome the main hurdles blocking his way and is left feeling secure that behind these secondary barriers he can satisfy his inquisitiveness.

Once inside the cubicle a mirror is presented in front of the viewer. A light is shone onto this mirror. All one can see is his reflection from the mirror. Money is inserted into a slot turning the *light off* inside the cubicle and *lighting up* the performance area behind the mirror. This cuts any reflection off the glass and a view through the one-way mirror is allowed. The interesting idea behind this mirror wall is that the performer cannot see to whom she is exhibiting herself for. The mirror wall acts as a one-way semi-penetrable screen. This furthers the anonymity of the customer but exploits the female of all her nudity. In the motion picture *Paris, Texas II,* the act of *being surveyed is* portrayed quite clearly; the footage of film where the customer, Harry Dean Stanton, can see the exhibit, Natassia

Kinski, inside the cubicle and could also communicate to her via a telephone. Kinski tries desperately to put a face to the voice; however, due to the nature of the non-permeable light screen on her side, she is unable. Again at the mercy of the voyeur.

The voyeur is very careful to maintain a void, and empty space, between the object and the eye, the object and his own body: *his look fixes the object and the eye at the correct distance.* The voyeur represents in space the fracture which forever separates him from the object; he represents his very dissatisfaction (which is what he requires as a voyeur), and also his satisfaction insofar as it is of a specifically voyeuristic type. To fill in this distance would threaten to overwhelm the subject, thus leading him to see the object – ie the object is too close for him to see it, to provide any pleasure of his own body, thus immobilising the senses of contact and putting an end to the scopic arrangement.

A processional route can be traced as each barrier is overcome, the *desire* to peep behind the mirrored wall becomes even greater. When the small cubicle space is entered the focal object, the eye, is used up in a transgression more daring than any that has preceded it. The rush of adrenaline stops, the curiosity is fulfilled satisfying the eagerness to a three dimensional cinema (see shop window displays) providing each voyeur with a personal thrill. As James Hillman in his account of voyeurism stated: 'There is an immense pleasure in watching. The senses are disassociated so that taste, touch and smell does not happen which is cut by the glass, so all that is left is the visual/optics. It intensifies all the sensations and sensuality going into the eye. . .'

James Hillman pointed out that, *there* is *a lot of pleasure* in *being able* to *see and not be seen* . . . The idea of fetishism has been identified by Jean Laplanche in his early encounter with the subject of 'Primal *Seduction'* by the reference he gives, that fundamental situations where the adult presents the infant with signifiers, non-verbal as well as verbal, and even behavioural, impregnated with unconscious sexual significations.

Confined to their Quarters
As she is the house for man she does not have one herself other than the one she constructs with her own decoration.   *Luce Irigaway, 1984*

One of man's greatest achievements has been via the conquest of his opposed gender. He has had to instigate clever ideals and laws, not only to dissolve her being as an *object d' art but* also to contain both her spiritual and physical presence *into* his domain.

Gender is a concept, undermined by a spatial logic that is masked in the moment of application to architecture, as an extra, or rather, prearchitectural given. The idea of feminine space is that of the structure of this mask. To examine this disguise means returning to the all too familiar scene of the patriarchal construction of the place of woman as the house. The introduction to a recent account on feminism and psychoanalysis describes how feminist theory domesticates itself inasmuch as it assumes a familial relationship to other treatise, like psychoanalysis, and focuses within that idea on 'private spaces.' Thus by doing so it occupies a 'stereotypically feminine space, *'placing itself in the sexualised, emotionalised, privatised, personalised sphere of the home and bedchamber rather than in the structure, impersonal, public realm.'*

Alberti's anthology, *On the Art of Building in Ten Books,* was crucial to its architectural promotion into the liberal arts. The fifth book, on discussing the design of 'private' houses, made unconcealed references to the patriarchal authority between spatial orders and a system of surveillance with implications to the gender. Women are to be confined deep within a sequence of spaces at the greatest distance *from* the outside world while men are to be exposed to that of the outside world; metamorphosing the house as a mechanism for the domestication of women. In Alberti's earlier discussion, *Della Famiglia,* the third book entitled 'Liber Tertius Familie: Economicus' (meaning the law of the household) does not appear to address architecture, other than discussing the position of the family house it:

'They used to say that men are by nature of a more elevated mind than women . . . The character of men is stronger than that of women and can bear the attacks of enemies better, can stand longer, is more constant under stress. Therefore men have the freedom to travel with honour in foreign lands. Women, on the hand, are almost all timid by nature, soft, slow, and therefore more useful when they sit still and watch over things . . . The woman, as she remains locked up at home, should watch over things by staying at her post . . . The man should guard the woman, the house and his family and country, but not by sitting still.'

Thus, what Alberti is proposing is that male mobility is assigned to the *outside* of the house and that the woman's position be assigned *within* the house. The spaces literally produce the effect of the gender, transforming the mental and physical character of those who occupy it. Alberti says if a role-reversal were to occur:
It would hardly win us respect if our wife busied herself among the man in the market place, out in the public eye. It also seems somewhat

demeaning to me to remain shut up in the house among women when I have manly things to do among men . . . Those idle creatures who stay all day among the little females or who keep their minds occupied with little feminine trifles certainly lack a masculine and glorious spirit . . . I believe that a man who is the father of a family not only should do all that is proper to a man, but that he must abstain from such activities as properly pertain to women.

Femininity is identified with spatial arrangements, the threat of being in the wrong place locates the man in the area of feminisation. However, if the woman were to go outside the house she would become *a more dangerous feminine* rather than more masculine. It was thought that the woman's interest in the outside put into question her chaste. The woman's sexuality would no longer be controlled by the house. The very mark of masculinity is due to the male's grasp on internal self control; it was as a result of this lack of self control that the Greeks thought woman were not to be trusted. The limits that state the interior of the person could not be supported by a woman because of her unstable sexuality endlessly overflowing and causing disruption, thus causing disorder to others, mostly men. Hence, the controlling of a woman could only be submission to an external law. She must be controlled by *being bounded,* marriage was instigated and idealised (understood as the domestication of a wild animal). *The role of architecture is explicitly in the control of sexuality within the security of the house,* here the woman's sexuality.

The social establishment of marriage is accustomised on the basis of spatial division of gender. As a result that the purpose of this institution is reproduction, which requires a shelter, a *roofed homestead,* making the marriage the sole reason for building a house. The word for the dweller of the house becomes 'husband', (originating from the word *oikos,* meaning household). While the home protects the children from the external elements, its primary role is to *protect the father's genealogical claims* by isolating women from other men. *Could this be a form of insecurity?* The law of the house is no more than the law of the father, he is the patriarchal master of the house.

However, a contradiction occurs here in that the man is immobile, he is fixed to the house, whereas the woman is mobile. Ann Carson argues this: At marriage the wife is taken not just (and perhaps not at all) into her husband's heart but into his house. This transgression is necessary (to legitimate contamination of the *oikos*), dangerous (insofar that the *oikos* incorporates a serious and permanent crisis of contact), and creates the context for illicit varieties of female mobility, for example that of the adulteress out of

FROM ABOVE: Soho Lights, 1993, London; plan of a London Peepshow 1993

her husband's house, with attendant damage to male property and reputation. The house is only operational if the woman is contained within it, without the threat of putting things out of place. It is only when the domestic routines are kept to its original spatial state that the house can literally provide the boundaries which control the female. The woman becomes woman-as-housed, such that her existence cannot be separated from the physical space.

Laura Mulvey's essay on Visual Pleasure, where she examines one of the contemporary forms of wall paintings – cinema, argues that: the gaze is masculine inasmuch it makes a subject's position occupying three-dimensional *Renaissance Space* and projecting itself at two dimensional surfaces of which the woman becomes one. Thus in this notion the female location is precisely not a position. The woman is not so much confined within the space as fetishically flattened into its surfaces. The space created is but an illusion . . . The viewer is constructed as a voyeur apparently detached from this illusion, looking into it, but looking precisely in order to see itself, as if in a mirror, occupying and controlling the space, which is to say, controlling its feminine surfaces.

The administration of the father, who governs the house, may be understood as the cross between spatial system and as a system of surveillance. When the role of the father is identified as the *'head of the household'* ('head' of the household is used as a mechanism to control the 'body' of the woman), Alberti uses the similarity of the spider whose own house is a mechanism for surveillance: You know the spider and how he constructs his web. All the threads sprayed out in rays, each of which, however long has its source, its roots, at the centre . . . The most industrious creature himself then sits at that spot and has his residence there. He remains in that place . . . and keeps so alert and watchful that if there is a touch on the finest and most distant threads he feels it instantly . . . and instantly takes care of the situation. Let the father of a family do likewise. Let him arrange his affairs and place them so that all look up too him . . . and by him attached to secure foundations.

Thus, placing the man in the centre of the family. The house is itself a way of looking, *a surveillance/ device* monitoring the possessions that occupy it: in that the walls displaying photographs, pictures, the enclosed spaces displaying and locating items collected over time and a standardised 'look' of each room. It is really the house, provided by the man, that

occupies his space, It is *his eye.* The wife merely maintains the very surveillance system she is placed in. She becomes one of the possessions monitored by the house which *she sustains.* She is *entrapped* by this system of class rather than the enclosure of the walls.

Just as the house is a machine for the domestication of woman, the house is also understood *as* the domesticated woman. Like the woman whose excessive sexuality is changed into productive work, it can become a substitute figure of control for the man. The house is itself feminine and can only become a surveillance mechanism when excesses have been controlled by the creator of such a mechanism, the *architect.*

The order of hierarchical spaces depends much upon the ordering of the body. Architecture was used to effect it as the agent of a new kind of inexcessivity and by doing so it played an active role in the establishment of the private subject. It clothed the body in a way that redefined it, at once making the body dangerous and containing that threat (see Josephine Baker's house). Thus, control of the body is an extension of the traditional disciplining of the woman, by the claim that she is much too much a 'fluid' body to control herself. The privatisation of sexuality, where sexuality is determined as feminine, is used to make the individual subject a *male subject and* subjectivity itself as masculine.

The establishment of masculine spaces was prescribed as the separation of bedrooms, where the female is only allowed to enter the husband's bedroom when permitted. The first truly male space was the study, a small locked room off his bedroom, which no one else was allowed to enter, an intellectual space, demeaning the wife's mental ability. The male is bestowed the space of spiritual knowledge whereas the female is given a dressing room, a confinement for material masks and pleasant odours. The study marks the internal boundary to the woman's authority within the house. She does not command the space. Her gaze only works between the inner locked door of the study and the outer locked door of the house. The study is seen as a truly male dominated area where the *master of the house* would keep his memoirs, notes on finance and other matters requiring the need to be in a private domain, away from the *harmful influence of Venus.*

Extracts from THE PERCEPTION OF SEEING by Jayesh Sidpara, Birmingham School of Architecture 1994.

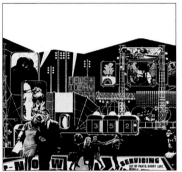

FROM ABOVE: Mannequins in Rakhams Department Store, 1992; Ron Herron, Instant City: Urban Action Tune Up, 1969

THE TEMPLE OF LAUGHTER

Laughter is the residue from a collapsed construction be it a story or of many storeys
The joke establishes a story for it to collapse with the punch line
Laughter then is the consummation of this collapse
From a condemned structure, a floor board, one seeks to bring down the House

The object in transit is locatable but has no location
Its precinct is always the present
The object does however have a site within which it is enclosed, the Envelope, and, if appropriately
wrapped, the object will be the Present
The Present arrives through the post
Yet until opened it doesn't belong anywhere or to anyone
It is an intention under wraps unseen and open only to speculation
The Envelope exposes the irony of opening
Once the ties are cut the site is tied to a precinct
Being of the floor in NW5 and on a flaw in LA

As required, the object is double wrapped
The Envelope doubles as a poster advertising a competition, which is a Double
The Temple of Laughter competition is held in England and due April Fools' day
As in Dostoevsky's double, THE END UP collapses notions of the authentic and the impostor
Each entry received for THE END UP is an echo of another competition
The sound of this echo is laughter

The entry submission hinges on the competition requirements and their subsequent collapse
The competition envelope describes a 12" X 12" X 12" model and a 36" X 36" drawing
Anything beyond the Envelope is outside the site boundaries
The model is able to collapse into the drawing
One finds it preferable then to build a drawing than to draw a building
Any Temple of Laughter is thus rendered laughable
The model comprises of 27 boxes, one for each letter of the alphabet so that each letter is assigned a
Letter Box
This box is assigned the grammatical period, the full stop
Defining this void are 26 Letter Boxes
When conected these letters make words and ultimately comprise sentences
As such, those found in competition rules adhered to the letter and were worshipped like shrines
Without a period a story becomes an interminable sentence
A life sentence where one man's laughter is another man's laughter

Anthony James Hoete with Yuji and Lee Hallman

*The programme of THE LAUGH was a Temple of Laughter. The competition was judged by Arthur
Erickson, Thom Mayne, Eric Owen Moss and Wolf D Prix and the winning and selected entries from
THE END's Second Annual Design Competition, THE LAUGH, were exhibited in the City of Los
Angeles from October 31, 1994– November 21, 1994. The winning design will be commissioned,
further developed and ultimately built in 1996.*

JASON GRIFFITHS, ALEX GINO, ED JESSON
London, England

The Temple of Laughter is derived from the maxim 'laughter makes laughter'. The phenomenon of laughter breeds laughter. It accelerates and compounds itself through its very existence in a way that all cognitive forms, written or symbolically understood are incapable of. The latter depends on your standpoint or cultural baggage while the sound of laughter has the potential to transcend representations of laughter understood by one group or another. Any attempt to codify laughter in terms of the dominant sense of humour risks discarding this thing that places it above any single language. The Temple of Laughter promotes the phenomenon of laughter through direct cohabitation with the architecture. It radiates laughter (through the walls), and then absorbs it (through the shrine).

Laughter wall: Touching the Tickler triggers laughter from the wall. The fitting and the architectural element are not mute. They are rigged and responsive to touch. Like the 'Artificial Sky' they are active and cannot be seen as silent components of architecture. The visitor proceeds through the space touches the Tickler and hears laughter. Different types of laughter are released depending on which section of the Tickler is touched.

Our site is a site of common experience. Our temple of Laughter places itself where it is most needed, whether it is Wilshire Boulevard, LA or Brent Cross London. The Temple of Laughter is a chance to plant the illogical within a framework of normality.

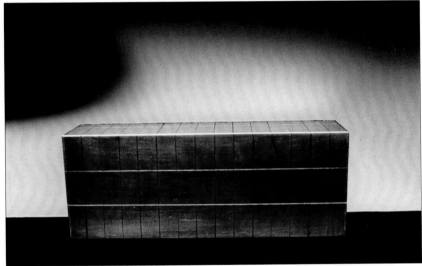

ANNA BARBARA

Imhof Austria

THE GAS TOWER: The temple which represents eternity does not exist anymore. Laugh is a moment and therefore exists as space which is not a space as such.

The Temple of Laughter consists of two spaces, the visual and the audial. Both exist just for moments if they get inhabited by people. Light represents the visual space of moment. When one person walks through the space of the Gas Tower he will strike sensors while moving through the space. These are connected with light beams. So as the person passes on his own way a couple of sensors, which are within the whole space but in his way, will generate his own Temple of Laughter: a space which will exist just for some moments like his laughter. Afterwards he is left in the space of the Gas Tower.

For the opening a special ceremony is proposed: Good laughing people will laugh into the tower to fill the space with energy. This laughter will be preserved like in a tin and replayed at the entrance and will fill the space of the Gas Tower. The person hears the immense delayed laughter when he touches a sensor, only for a moment. But the laughter vanishes until it has lost its energy. This is a loss indicated by the loss of the lightpower.

So either this space gets filled up with new energy, people laughing in the visual space of light or the audial and visual space, which both are connected through human perception and interacting, or the Temple will stop existing.

The delay of 15 seconds of voices in the Gas Tower catches the laugh for moments.

The shrine is the human being himself and it will stop existing in its function in his space with the dematerialisation of the Temple.

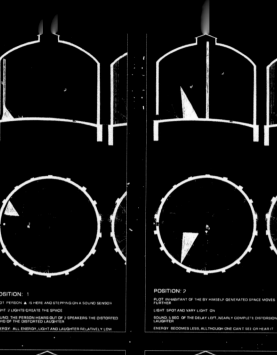

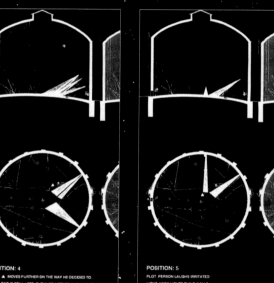

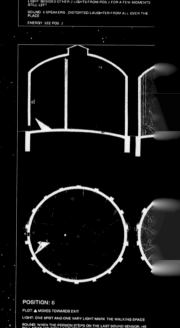

JUNYA TODA
Osaka, Japan

In Japan, Osaka is generally known as the birthplace of 'Comedy Culture' and plays an important role even now. The essence of 'Laugh' is seen on the exaggerated signboards of commercial buildings along 'The Dotonbori River' in the centre of Osaka. The site of the Temple is located here. The Temple embodies a gigantic 'L' and 'H' from the word 'Laugh' which has no meaning in itself. At the site, the architecture is totally composed of two walls, slabs, zigzagged frame and void space. Walls are twisted diagonally and hollowed in 'L' and 'H' figures. It could be said that the architecture involves triple vacancy in the midst of a noisy city.

On the street, people will see the big signboard of unfinished concrete and then enter the interior open-air space, where floors made of bent walls of the signboard build a labyrinth. A person will twist his body to fit the complicated space and climb upwards where he thinks the 'Shrine' might be. But finally, after excessive strain he will find nothingness.

Between the two walls or in the middle of two and three dimensions he will, unconsciously, be an entertainer on the screen; that is to say he will be the 'Shrine' itself and fill the vacancy while people are laughing at his face of confusion and his twisted body like the figure of the 'Temple'. However, he will have the last laugh when he becomes aware of what the vacancy of life means.

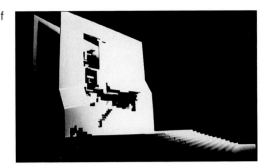

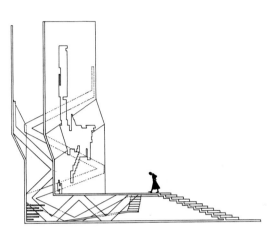

VISEGRÁD CAMP, HUNGARY

IMRE MAKOVECZ

The Hungarian organic architect, Imre Makovecz's soaring wooden vaults and sinuous organic forms stand apart from the anonymous architecture produced by the Hungarian State department and the freedom that it represents has caused him to become the 'people's hero' in Hungary. In the West he has been widely praised for his sensitivity to the site and his ability to create architecture 'with a soul' while in Hungary, it is more difficult to get an appointment to see Makovecz than it is to get an interview with the president. Recently, however, Makovecz has come across serious opposition. The root of the problem lies in the answer to the following paradox: why, when Makovecz was chosen by the Ministry of International Economic Relations of the Hungarian Republic to represent his country by designing the Hungarian Pavilion for the 1992 Seville Expo, are some of the most inspirational projects in Hungary with which Makovecz has been involved, being threatened with demolition? Why the extraordinary change of heart?

Although different governments have obviously reacted differently to Makovecz, he emphatically denies that the State has had any hand in the threat to demolish his buildings at Visegrád. However the political situation cannot be ignored. After a period of progressively more democratic government in the late 80s and early 90s, the 'renamed' Socialist party had a landslide victory in May 1994. That this coincides with the Pilis forestry company's threat to destroy Makovecz's buildings may be a coincidence. Makovecz believes that the Pilis' change in attitude under new leadership is responsible but admits that 'in the background there are hidden the most antisocial ulterior motives'.

The Pilis forestry company on whose land the Visegrád buildings are located, claims that the structures have no planning permission and that they are 'ugly, dangerous and disordered'. Under previous leadership, Pilis commissioned Makovecz to build the Cultural Centre (1976-81) for the site and, in 1981, allowed him to use the disused stone pit for his student summer camp. As for 'dangerous', according to Makovecz the students of the next camp would make any repairs Pilis deemed necessary. Permission and safety aside, the only answer is what Makovecz

describes as 'pseudo-official arguments' and what Christopher Day (the British organic architect and author of 'Places for the Soul') recognises as 'the conspiracy of the "Greys"'. It is particularly revealing that Pilis described the buildings as 'ugly'. Makovecz's forms are indeed powerful symbols of creative resistance in striking contrast to the State department's soulless Soviet style concrete buildings. Indeed, it seems that Pilis is alone on this – one British guide book to Hungary warns 'We should also point out right away that the houses that are built in rural areas nowadays are just plain hideous.'

Makovecz organised the Visegrád student camps because he believes that 'The future of architecture is not a theoretical question, the future of architecture is the architectural students at the universities'. This philosophy has international implications and together with the Hungarian 'living architecture' group, 'Kos Karoly', Makovecz has already run several projects at the Prince of Wales Institute of Architecture in London. However he has concentrated most of his efforts on Budapest Technical University which places a soul destroying emphasis on theory. The University's approach means that the students lack practical training, are discouraged from social interaction and the course fails to fulfil their spiritual needs.

Through the summer camp, Makovecz discovered that – 'the students are eager to be competitive. They gladly discuss which is the best project and are ready to support it even if the author is someone else and they have to learn to be the loser'. Makovecz 'living architecture' is an architecture of participation rather than of observation. As with other projects, his limited budgets mean that the community who commission the project also build it which makes the final form a manifestation of the spirit of that community, its people and the genius loci.

The Visegrád student work is, in Makovecz's opinion, a 'model for human settlement'. The buildings include: a place of pilgrimage, the Hive (1981); a physical shelter, the Cave (1982); the connection between man made roads, the Bridge (1982-83); the desire to reach beyond ourselves manifested in the Tower (1985); the entry into the external world expressed through the Sign (1986); the knowledge of astrological

OPPOSITE FROM ABOVE: The Dancing Barn, 1987; The Pod, 1988

FROM ABOVE L to R: The Hive,
1981; The Tower, 1985; The
Cave, 1982-83; The Bridge,
1982-83

order evident in the design and orientation of the Barn (1987) and the discovery of the individual nature of the self through the Pod (1988).

From first impressions, some people might describe the Visegrád buildings as follies. Indeed a well known English critic recently accused Makovecz of 'wilful individualism'. Makovecz sees the issue of their worth in another manner – 'I think there is no sense at all in pulling them down, for this would show that there was no understanding of the purpose of the camp.' Surely, the purpose is in the quest for communication between human beings, a communication that can only come about if architecture transcends the realm of the functional and fulfils its psychological and educational obligations? But apart from their symbolic value, the buildings are important to the Hungarian State for a wide variety of commercial, cultural and technical reasons:

From a technical point of view, the Visegrád 'earth architecture' is all constructed using natural materials of wood and earth and the structures anticipate the importance of natural light and ventilation by their aspect and the strategic placing of openings. The Cave, for example, is a pseudo cupola made from leftover planks nailed together and covered in soil and punctuated by openings which draw air through. The Hive is a bell-like shape whose essential structure relies on 24 bent saplings. Natural light enters from strategically placed openings. It could be argued that, as products of living architecture, Makovecz should accept that his Visegrád camp constructions have a finite life. However, that a thing is living does not mean that it should be prematurely destroyed and indeed the living process includes decay and repair. So is the camp valuable from an architectural point of view? Jonathan Glancey has described Makovecz's work as 'the most environmentally responsive or green architecture to be found anywhere'.

From a commercial angle, 10 to 15 thousand people come from Budapest to the Visegrád tourist centre. Makovecz's work offers an alternative to the disappointingly 'kitsch' 'Tschikosch, Goulash and Fogas'-tourism that, in the long term, is detrimental to the Hungarian tourist trade. Makovecz is deeply nationalist and believes that re-identification will emerge from the genuinely indigenous roots of his country. The 'Dancing Barn', is an excellent 'living' example of the strong tradition of anthropomorphic architecture in Hungary. 'Its body was made from the forest; its ribs were carved of wood. Made sentient and agitated, the creature was set on its feet'. Makovecz's buildings give the impression of coming alive. This thatched hut gives the feeling of protection and space. The supporting tree trunks around the edge leave an uninterrupted area for performers who can also make use of the subtly enhanced auditorium-like topography of one area of the site which is the Theatre (1989).

Visegrád is situated on one of the most beautiful bends of the Danube and tourists are encouraged to rediscover a 'conscious contact with nature'. Makovecz often uses allegories to describe his philosophy. He claims that 'The real problem is that people don't perceive that they part of Nature ... If I can't see the difference between an oak and a beech, it doesn't mean that they are the same but that my ignorance prevents me from seeing their difference.' On a practical level, the Tower, comprised of three braced wooden trunks, provides a viewing platform. From a more abstract but equally valuable point of view, the 'unconscious inspiration' from which the sinuous organic forms: Road (1984), Sign, Pod and Circle (1990) are derived, is reminiscent of the increasingly influential Land Art movement's site responsive sensitivity. This universal need to re-identify with nature provides important cultural links with the rest of Europe and America.

Student camps such as the Visegrád project mean little in western Europe, but they are of enormous importance in Hungary where building has played a greater part in the search for re-identification than in anywhere else in the Soviet block. Although we might place more value on Makovecz's Seville Expo building because of its physical scale, polished craftsmanship and high international profile, in Hungary, Visegrád is far more important. This is the fundamental reason for the 'change of heart'. After an abortive State competition for an Expo design, Makovecz's knowledge of traditional organic Hungarian architecture meant he was the obvious choice to represent hungary. Makovecz uses traditional themes, appropriate for a 'representative' building but he uses them not for aesthetic reasons but to encourage re-identification and resist conformity by developing positive and original designs. To non-Hungarians, the Expo design did not seem to challenge the status quo. The building has since been bought by a commercial technology company and converted into offices so even the subtle significance it had is in the past. For Hungarians, however, the Visegrád camp is a living symbol of hope for the future.

Katherine MacInnes

Constructive comments can be addressed to the head of the Pilis forestry company: István Dobó (Managing Director), Pilisi Parkerdo, Részvénytársaság, Mátyás Király U 4, Hungary.

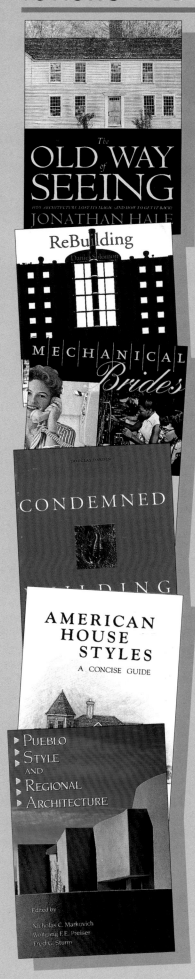

OLD WAY OF SEEING How Architecture Lost its Magic (and how to get it back), Jonathan Hale, 241pp, b/w ills, £15.99 HB
Hale works from the premise that old buildings have a natural grace which is rare in new buildings. He explores the transition from architecture as an expression of the human spirit to an architecture laden with symbols. By isolating the features he considers to be responsible for animating beautiful buildings Hale attempts to show how we can repair the built environment. Like other traditionalists Hale is trying to prove that beauty is encapsulated in certain elements which can be universally appreciated. However the ratio between the universal or objective fact and the subjective assumption still remains. Some chapters have an air of empiricism, for example, the section on mystery and the rules of proportion while others are obviously coloured by American nationalism. Hale concludes that a return to traditional values in architecture can only be achieved by rediscovering our powers of intuition to re-enter the 'old way of seeing'.

ReBUILDING by Daniel Solomon, Princeton Architectural Press, 142pp, b/w ills, PB
In *ReBuilding*, San Francisco–based architect and town planner Daniel Solomon puts forth his views on the current state of American sub/urban design. The first part of this book, 'Words', describes Solomon's ideas about the city and the ways in which he believes the process of making towns has gone 'haywire.' Part two, 'Works', contains built projects and plans by the architect including House for Two Musicians, Amancio Ergina Village, and Hayward Downtown Plan. Together, Solomon's words and works provide alternative solutions to the problems he sees developing in the new growth areas, both urban and suburban, of this country. Along with architects like Peter Calthorpe, Andres Duany, and Elizabeth Plater-Zyberk, Daniel Solomon has been at the forefront of a movement which seeks to repair the blighted American townscape. His first book, *ReBuilding* is an important contribution to this new way of thinking about town planning.

MECHANICAL BRIDES Women and Machines from Home to Office by Ellen Lupton, Princeton University Press, 65pp, £NA PB
We know that design affects every aspect of our daily life but it is interesting to reverse this maxim to analyse 'zeitgeist' or the spirit of the age from designed objects. Cultural ideas about duties and ambitions of women are reflected and reinforced by the ways appliances have been designed, marketed, used and imagined. The illustrations reveal the gender significance attached to seemingly neutral things. Texts by feminist historians of technology and design 'revise the fairy-tale narrative in which household appliances rescue American women from domestic drudgery'. Indeed by glamorising appliances as partners in achieving health and happiness, advertising and design have encouraged women to embrace housework as women's 'natural calling'. While office equipment was romanticised, the similarity between the piano and the typewriter was used by manufacturers and employers to suggest that women's agility and musicality make them natural typists.

CONDEMNED BUILDING by Douglas Darden, Princeton University Press, 160pp, b/w ills, PB
This presents ten rhetorical projects conceived as buildings that are 'condemned from the start'. Each project comprises exquisite drawings and model photographs, as well as a psychodramatic text. Darden's projects, with names such as Museum of Impostors and Clinic for Sleep Disorders, form a treatise on the nature of unfulfilled desire. The Museum of Impostors exhibits stories of the lives of individuals in American history who have pretended to be someone different all their lives. The building is a half-bridge in the Baltimore Harbour Water Gap. Darden has conceived of The 'Night School' designated no longer as a place of learning between students and teachers, instead it is a place in which to watch performance and movies.

AMERICAN HOUSE STYLES A Concise Guide by John Milnes Baker, WW Norton and Company, 190pp, b/w ills, US$19.95 HB

This unique book will allow readers to recognise the architectural features and style of virtually any house they encounter. Each section begins with a historical overview of the period, followed by a concise commentary of each style. The author then highlights the specific design that distinguishes one style from another. He shows how different styles developed and what influenced their development. The elevation drawings throughout, accompanied by floor plans, illustrate the details of style clearly and with precision, allowing one to see what is meant by 'Federal', 'Italianate' 'Spanish Mission' etc which make up the history of American domestic architecture. All this is achieved by the author/architect designing a two-storey house with four bedrooms, from which the basic plan is developed in almost any number of historical styles. By this technique, the essential characteristics of a given style can be emphasised in each version of the house. The result is a critical assessment of the man-made world and, through an understanding of earlier styles, gives a considered and informed insight into the architecture of the present day.

PUEBLO STYLE AND REGIONAL ARCHITECTURE edited by Nicholas C Markovich, Wolfgang FE Preiser and Fred G Sturm, Van Nostrand Reinhold, 1989, 348pp, b/w ills, £32.50 HB
Taking an architectural, artistic, archaeological, anthropological, philosophical and historical perspective, Pueblo style is considered not simply architecturally but within its cultural, religious, economic and climatic contexts as well – to an understanding of the 'mystique of New Mexico'. The product of successive layers of Pueblo Indian, Spanish and Anglo influences, contemporary Pueblo style is above all seen as a harmonious response to the magnificent landscape from which it emerged. *Pueblo Style and Regional Architecture* examines Pueblo Indian concepts of space, form and aesthetics. It traces the historical evolution of an indigenous American architecture, from prehistoric Anasazi settlements to the appearance of Mogollon pit houses. It also introduces the developments

that occurred during the Spanish colonisation through to the modern Pueblo communities. The architecture is seen as a revivalist phenomenon, and in conjunction with land is seen as a 'romantic' influence in the work of the region's best known Anglo artist, Georgia O'Keeffe.

BUILDING THE WEST RIDING A Guide to its Architecture and History by Lynn F Pearson, Smith Settle Limited, 223pp, b/w and col ills, £11.95 PB, £16.95 HB
Covering a large part of Yorkshire, from Sedbergh in the north to Sheffield in the south, from Goole in the east to Huddersfield in the west, this book leads the reader through an explorative, historical journey of the area's built heritage – from abbeys (Fountains Abbey) and aqueducts to breweries and bridges, mills and manor houses (Newby Hall) to temples and towers (the Victorian towers of Allerton Park). Aimed primarily for the traveller, this book tries to answer the question: 'Why does it look like that?', by evaluating the financial, topographical, political and fashionable aspects which influence the history of the West Riding and its architecture, and the influences which have shaped the facades. Not meant as a comprehensive textbook, this publication introduces the reader to the architectural history of the area explaining how and why the buildings came to be, leaving the traveller to see for themselves the surprise, the puzzlement that the buildings offer.

LANDSCAPE DESIGN WITH PLANTS Second Edition edited by Brian Clouston for the Landscape Institute, 1990, 416pp, b/wills, £25.00 PB
Divided into two parts, this book is planned for landscape architects and those concerned with planting design, that is the creation of a 'second world', within the natural world, by design. This is becoming especially interesting with the considerable technical innovations and widening of the range and variety of landscape projects undertaken in parts of the world where climate, culture and native flora offer new opportunities – and pose new problems. The first part discusses design with plants as

the *raison d'être* of technique, following the British tradition of incorporating intellectual and emotional values into the process of forming man-made landscapes. The second part concerns the techniques to be used in the modern application of landscape design with plants, and hence has been revised and updated to make available contemporary knowledge and thought about the subject. Combined, these two parts offer a comprehensive, theoretical and practical book covering all aspects of landscape design with plants.

STRUCTURE & ARCHITECTURE by Angus J MacDonald, Butterworth Heineman Ltd, 131pp, b/w ills, £14.95 PB
Different building types demonstrate that all buildings contain a structure, the function of which is to support the building envelope by conducting the forces which are applied to it from the points where they arise in the building to the ground below it where they are ultimately resisted. The structural elements of engineering are considered, namely stability which is dependent on the geometric configuration of the structure and therefore is a consideration that affects the determination of its form; the structural materials – masonry, timber, steel and concrete; and structural arrangements – post-and-beam, semi-form-active and fully-form-active. By focusing on these elements the author highlights that the principal objective of engineering design is to provide an object which will function satisfactorily with maximum economy of means.

WHAT IS ARCHITECTURE An Essay on Landscapes, Buildings, and Machines by Paul Shepheard, 131pp, b/w ills, £7.95 PB
At a time when it is fashionable to say that architecture is everything – from philosophy to science to art to theory – Shepheard boldly and irreverently sets limits to the subject in quasi novelistic style complete with characters and dialogue but no plot. Using a narrative form, he takes strong positions, names the causes of the problems and tells us how bad things are and how they can prepare. Instead of the usual claims or complaints, Shepheard uses a contiguous form

of argument to discuss observations of an altogether different order examining the question of Architecture as a metaphor, or Architecture as a computer program.

FETISH edited by Sarah Whiting, Edward Mitchell and Greg Lynn, Princeton University Press 173pp, b/w ills, £NA HB
Marx, Adorno, Benjamin and Baudrillard have all used the term 'fetish' in reference to the commodity culture resulting from a capitalist economy and society. Freud defined the term as 'a substitute which blocks or displaces a traumatic discovery of loss'. Like Jeffrey Kipnis in his essay 'Freudian Slippers' many people will be suspicious of 'architecture borrowing yet another concept for commodification from the so-called strong disciplines of psychoanalysis, literary criticism and philosophy.' Yet the definition of Fetish as an oxymoron, a situation where the conventional becomes unique is a thought provoking one. In his essay 'Theoretical Slippage' Mark Wigley introduces a second factor which is that we are all subjects of fetishism since as Freud says in his 'Three Essays on the Theory of Sexuality' – 'A certain degree of fetishism is . . . habitually present in normal love'.

THE CLASSICAL VERNACULAR Architectural Principles in an Age of Nihilism by Roger Scruton, Carcanet Press, 157pp, b/w ills, £19.95 HB
Roger Scruton argues that 'vulgar tongue' that is the vernacular tradition is the natural language of space, proportion and light. One of the most interesting essays Art History and Aesthetic judgement tackles the problem of subjectivity. He works from contrasting premises that aesthetic judgement could be interpreted as untutored judgement or as requiring a method – either position involves subjectivity. He also describes the origin of Art history quoting Wölfflin's 'Principles of Art History' who claimed that 'To explain a style cannot mean anything but to fit its expressive character into the general history of the period, to prove that its forms do not say anything in their language that is not also said by the other organs of the age'.

WORLD CITIES

World Cities is a prestigious series about prominent cities of the world, stemming from the vital and poignant need to consider our urban environment in the latter part of the twentieth century. The series presents a detailed and intelligent analysis of the state of the world's cities and their visions of the future. It will examine not only the social environment and planning history of each city, but projects that were never realised: the missed opportunities that might have created a city with a very different atmosphere. A comprehensive collection of essays, illustrations and projects representing the gamut of architectural styles gives this series a unique viewpoint. Other forthcoming issues of this series include Berlin, Tokyo, New York and Barcelona.

BERLIN
World Cities III
Edited by Alan Balfour

Alan Balfour presents a remarkable overview of a city in a state of architectural flux, undergoing a massive urban restructuring and renewal. The projects featured begin just before the fall of the Wall, with the IBA competitions. They go on to chart the progress of major competitions and buildings generated by the new unity – for the Potsdamer Platz, the Reichstag, Spreebogen, Alexander Platz and World Trade Centre. Certain trends emerge, from the awe inspiring visions of Morphosis, Libeskind and Zaha Hadid to the cool order of Kleihues and Kollhoff. The work of many German and international architects is featured.

A photographic essay introduces the *Berlin*, showing the city as it was between the Wars. Dr Hans Stimmann, Daniel Libeskind, Axel Schultes and Christoph Langhof present their ideas for the city's future. This is followed by three project sections: 'Berlin as it Might Have Been', which shows schemes and competition entries which remain unrealised; 'Berlin as

it is', presenting projects which are complete or under construction; and 'Berlin as it Will be', featuring schemes which will be completed in the future. Alan Balfour introduces each section with incisive critical essays. Finally, a map places each of the schemes in its urban context.

Hardback 1 85490 374 8
305 x 252 mm, 400 pages
Over 700 illustrations, mainly in colour
April 1995

LONDON
EDITED BY KENNETH POWELL

HB 1 85490 188 5
305 x 252 mm, 416 pages,
Extensively illustrated in colour
Publication: 1993

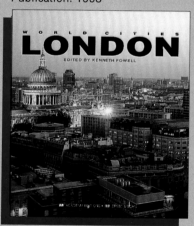

LOS ANGELES
HB 1 85490 293 8
305 x 252mm, 400 pages
Over 730 illustrations, mainly in colour
Publication: 1994

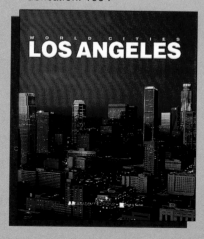

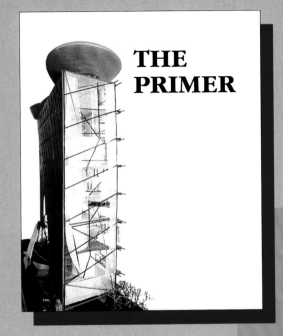

THE PRIMER

This clear, concise text, derived from a series of lectures and written by one of the founder members of Archigram, highlights the many challenges faced by an architect today. Peter Cook dissects the building into individual elements, such as staircases, entrance halls and living areas and describes the design concept of each subject in detail. From this point he goes on to discuss the wider implications of design and its theory, enabling the reader to build up an understanding of the whole project by a knowledge of its parts. Numerous examples, from many architects including Lebbeus Woods, Morphosis, Itsuko Hasegawa, Eric Owen Moss and Coop Himmelb(l)au, and many engaging explanations provide an informative and lively text for both 1st and 2nd year students and beyond.

Paperback 1 85490 388 8
217 x 279 mm 128 pages
Illustrated throughout
Publication: March 1995

Modernism has dominated architectural theory and practice for most of the 20th century. The International Style, which emerged at the beginning of this century partly as a reaction against Victorian high style, produced many sleek, elegant buildings. The architectural reaction to this incredible social movement which swept through all aspects of society was to provide good, low-cost public housing. It has achieved a worldwide undeniable influence whether for good or bad and continues to influence many architects today. This, the fourth in our 'What is' series explains Modernism in an illuminating and accessible style. Many examples are used to illustrate this movement, from the large scale public architecture through the many utopian housing schemes, to the private houses illustrating the many masterpieces created during this period. Among the many buildings featured are Mies van der Rohe's Seagram Building, New York, and Farnsworth House, Illinois; Mendelsohn & Chermayoff's Bexhill Pavilion, England; Le Corbusier's Villa Savoye, France, and Unite D'habitation, Marseilles. The text provides a lively and informative analysis of the subject and covers many aspects of Modernism, including the art and culture of this fascinating period.

Paperback 1 85490 389 6
240 x 255 mm 68 pages
Extensively illustrated, mainly b/w
Publication: 1995

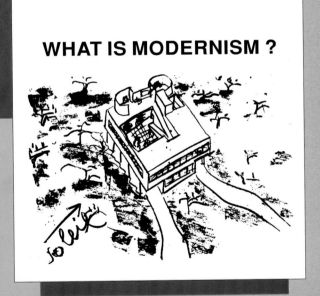

WHAT IS MODERNISM ?

Further information can be obtained from Academy Group Ltd. Tel: 071 402 2141 Fax: 071 723 9540

ELSPETH BEARD
WATER TOWER
Munstead

Elspeth Beard won the 1994 Downland Design Award for her conversion of the Munstead Water Tower in Godalming, Surrey into a home. Beard spent five years on the conversion. She wanted to live somewhere which had not originally been designed as a house and which provided the freedom to design the living space as she wished. She carried out much of the building work herself, and provided all the finances for the project.

The original grade II listed 130-foot octagonal brick tower was constructed in 1898 and was in use for approximately 70 years. It had been derelict for nearly 20 years when it was sold by Thames Water in October 1988. The conversion consists of six floors, each of which is comprised of one octagonal room approximately 25 feet across and 16 feet high. There is a reception room/all on the ground floor, one bedroom on each of the first, second and third floors, a kitchen dining room on the fourth floor and a living room within the old tank room on the fifth floor. Four of the floors have mezzanine galleries: each of the bedrooms has a bathroom on the mezzanine.

Beard designed the interior to retain as much of the original building as possible. The tank base now provides a steel riveted ceiling to the kitchen. The 20-foot float and valve, which were originally in the tank now provide a feature for the fifth-floor living room. Stairs to each floor wrap round the Tower, bolted the inside of the exterior wall. A cast iron spiral staircase links the kitchen and living room – making a total of 142 steps in the Tower.

ARCHITECTURE & WATER

NICHOLAS GRIMSHAW, BRITISH PAVILION EXPO '92, SEVILLE

Architectural Design

ARCHITECTURE & WATER

RICARDO LEGORRETA, HOTEL REGINA, CANÇUN; *OPPOSITE*: TADAO ANDO, WATER TEMPLE, HONPUKUJI

ACADEMY EDITIONS · LONDON

Acknowledgements

All material is courtesy of the authors and architects unless otherwise stated.
'The Potential For Wonder', is reprinted from *Water and Architecture* by Charles Moore and Jane Lidz.
Published in 1994 by Harry N Abrams, In., NewYork. All Rights Reserved.
We are grateful to The Groninger Museum, Groningen for providing images of the completed building.
The text for Tadao Ando Water Temple is adapted from the book *From Shinto To Ando: Studies in Architectural Anthropology in Japan*, Günter Nitschke, Academy Editions, London, 1993.

Front Cover: Shoei Yoh, Prospecta '92, Toyama; *Inside Covers:* Moore Ruble Yudell, Kobe Nishiokamoto, Kobe, Japan; *Back Cover:* Philip Larkin, Water

Photographic Credits
Front Cover and *p48* Y Takase; *pp2 and 81* Hiroshi Ueda; *p19 above and centre* Iris Water and Design; *p19 below* Mälmo Flowforms; *pp22, 24, 25 and 27 below* Timothy Hursley; *pp30 and 31* van der Vulgt & Claus; *pp32-35* Tom Bonner; *pp36-38* William Pye; *p41* Paul Warchol; *pp58 and 59 above left* Jim Hedrich; *p59* L Legorreta; *pp59, 60 and 61 below right* James Wilson; *pp72 and 73 below and centre left* C Dow; *p75 above right* Lawrence Manning; *p75 below right* G Crawford; *pp76 and 80* Tadao Ando; *pp82, 84, 85 and 86* Richard Davies; *p87 below* Richard Davies and Tom Miller; *p91 above* Eamonn O'Mahony; *p92 above* Matthew Antrobi

EDITOR: Maggie Toy
EDITORIAL TEAM: Iona Spens, Katherine MacInnes, Stephen Watt
ART EDITOR: Andrea Bettella CHIEF DESIGNER: Mario Bettella DESIGNER: Toby Norman

CONSULTANTS: Catherine Cooke, Terry Farrell, Kenneth Frampton, Charles Jencks, Heinrich Klotz, Leon Krier, Robert Maxwell, Demetri Porphyrios, Kenneth Powell, Colin Rowe, Derek Walker

First published in Great Britain in 1995 by *Architectural Design* an imprint of
ACADEMY GROUP LTD, 42 LEINSTER GARDENS, LONDON W2 3AN
Member of the VCH Publishing Group
ISBN: 1 854 90 2474 (UK)

Architectural Design Profile 113 is published as part of *Architectural Design* Vol 65 1-2/1995
Architectural Design Magazine is published six times a year and is available by subscription

Distributed to the trade in the United States of America by
ST MARTIN'S PRESS, 175 FIFTH AVENUE, NEW YORK, NY 10010

Printed and bound in Italy

Contents

ARCHITECTURAL DESIGN PROFILE No 113
ARCHITECTURE & WATER

EDITORIAL
Maggie Toy

Water has always been imperative for life and the genesis of settlement. Its integration within architecture has assumed many forms and served many purposes. Water's traditional role in strategic defence is legendary, but the protective capacity of this ambiguous element must be balanced against its inherent danger. This is encapsulated in the concept of the moat, which was designed to protect those within but equally made the inhabitants vulnerable to siege. The innate force within water represents the essence of Yin and Yang where good cannot exist without evil.

The forces of iced and stable water have been responsible for sculpting many of the world's landscapes through glaciers, seas, rivers and precipitation; so when designers embark upon integrating architecture and water there is a precedent set by nature as well as a force that needs to be harnessed. Shoei Yoh demonstrates the incredible beauty of the 'creation of weather' with his *Prospecta '92* in Toyama, where advanced technology is used to instigate 'weather' diversities within the confines of the structure.

The power and force of water contribute to the dynamic of the architecture which incorporates it. An extreme example of this is the Hoover Dam which hovers across the mountains in Nevada, Arizona, demonstrating its strength in containing the huge pressure of water stacked behind it. The control that is inflicted upon the water creates a tension, both visual and actual, which is provocative and disturbing. This same concept can be used within the more accessible features of an architectural vocabulary. Steven Holl's manipulation of a stream through the Stretto House in Texas demonstrates a subtle control which is more indicative of working with this force, as opposed to overcoming it. The principle of control is also implemented in the installation of a swimming pool, illustrated by the pool at the Adelphi Hotel in Melbourne, by Denton Corker Marshall, which is crafted in glass, placed on top of a high rise, and projects slightly so that it appears to defy the laws of gravity. This effect challenges our perception, in terms of the weight carried by the structure and the transparency of both the water and glass, capturing the imagination of the viewer and the user.

Another dichotomy which is embedded within the influence of water is its power to tranquillise. The use of water within architecture is often used to illicit a peaceful response within the project. The inclusion of water in the landscapes of artist Ian Hamilton Finlay, demonstrates how the implementation of water enlarges the effective area. He describes the scheme as 'an inland garden where evocations of the sea are omnipresent . . . where trees will conjure up the sounds of adjacent water'. Artist and sculptor Andy Goldsworthy, on the other hand, tries to tap the energy of water, frozen and otherwise, as a vital part of the nature which he manipulates, sympathetically, in his art. His work illustrates the versatility and vitality of the element within nature.

Water's reflective properties, along with the audiovisual effects of moving water, offers architects a tool for creating energy and space. Most people can be seduced by the burbling brook phenomenon, that beguiling quality created by water. The popularity of fountains all over the world clearly demonstrates its mass appeal; an appeal which is frequently harnessed by architects.

Julian Jones provides a detailed assessment of the processes and influences that the use of water has upon the architectural profession. He explains the increasing demands to 'make water work' in order to meet the ever growing expectations for high environmental standards at a reasonable cost. Jones outlines the unique physical and chemical properties of the substance and how these are being used to enhance the quality of life.

The relationship between water and architecture inevitably poses many structural problems. Water's inclusion in a scheme usually creates a weak point within the design. Considerable time is spent detailing buildings to keep water out and the problems that arise when a volume of water is introduced into a scheme are no less difficult. This issue reveals how the development of the expertise necessary for this, combined with the use of advances in technology, in conjunction with the psychological benefits of water, can be used effectively working towards the ideal integration of architecture and its dynamic component, water.

OPPOSITE: Shoei Yoh, Prospecta '92, Toyama. Advanced technology is used to create weather within a specific framework; ABOVE: Denton Corker Marshall, The Adelphi Hotel, Melbourne. The overhanging pool's transparent qualities challenge perception.

AARON BETSKY
TAKE ME TO THE WATER
Dipping in the History of Water in Architecture

The *locus classicus* for the use of water in architecture is the Alhambra. Here a variety of pools, fountains and irrigation channels enchains the delicacies of architecture in a network of connections, reflections and elaborations that come close to bridging the separations made by architecture. For, if buildings divorce us from nature, both to protect us from the elements and to erect a more rational human realm in its stead, and if they then replace our bodies with a second, alien form that, though designed in our image, is cold and removed, the sensual play of water reconnects us. In the Alhambra and the gardens of the Generalife the heat is softened by something ephemeral, rather than being cut out by walls. A new Eden surrounds you with trees, bushes and flowers whose presence flows from the water. In the entry court, a small burble of water heightens the clean serenity of cool stone pavers. Power and place centre in the Court of the Lions, and distribute their beneficence to define the edges of the courtyard. Gravity turns into a narrative of connecting channels and pools that guide you through space. The pool's surface in the Court of Myrtles doubles forms, muddles distinctions and continues a decorative activity that weaves all together, rather than creating distinctions. It is not just the eye that delights; the coolness of the air, the scents of fresh water and even the implied touch of water on the skin convert the buildings from something seen by expert eyes – the judge of all architecture in Western culture – into something sensed by the body.

There are other monuments to the connective capabilities of water, such as the gardens of the Villa d'Este in Tivoli or of the Taj Majal in Agra, but the function of water in architecture does not need such showplaces to work its wonders. In some cases, water is so integrated into the built fabric that it cannot be distinguished from the built form. Such is certainly the case in that other reference point of aquatic form Venice, but it is also true in the more mundane forms of The Netherlands. There, the presence of water has shaped the whole character of the environment. In fact, the word 'landscape' is a word brought over by William and Mary's gardeners to describe what the Dutch had been doing since the time of the

Romans: taking a swamp that faded from river to sea with little stable ground in between and converting it into arable, usable land.[1] The continual battle against the sea and the need to create irrigation projects created a political tradition of localized cooperation and entrepreneurship that allowed Holland to avoid the excesses of feudalism and nationalism. This economic logic evidenced itself in the grids of irrigation canals and the labyrinthine appearance of the concentric canals built around the dam that gave Amsterdam its name. An art of representation whose foundation is the control of nature and its artful exhibition, what Svetlana Alpers has called a 'Northern mode of picture making' in which 'seeing is knowing is making', has as its basis the control and use of water for agriculture and commerce.[2]

These are the two poles of an aquatic architecture. On the one hand, architecture is a sensual element added to the act of construction that heals the irreparable wound created by the very act of building, while on the other hand it is a necessary element that develops the character of the built environment in economically logical ways. Beyond these fundamental functions, there are only myths; water as the continuum of the universe made real, water as the source of life and rebirth, water as the mirror that creates a heterotopic alternative to lived experience. These mythic dimensions inform the uses of water in the architecture, but are not contained by them. When fountains try to embody them, as was the vogue from the masque of the 16th century to the architecture *parlante* of Ledoux's saltworks at Arc-et-Senans, they are only illustrative, leaving the true power of water to overwhelm their stories with splashing delight or nourishing drinks.[3]

The mythic meanings of architecture are of course myriad. It is first and foremost another world, both purer and inaccessible. Atlantis exists underwater, and when you are baptised you are reborn as a pure Christian. It is also the crossing place to another world where the body cannot follow; the Styx, Ganges and Nile all take one to the world of the dead. Floating within it, there is continuity: water is the Christian symbol of bounty and the Cretan sign for life itself. It is the water that, per Heraclitus, is never the same. Once contained, it gives life,

Shoei Yoh, Arashiyama Golf Club, Okinawa Island

by providing something to drink, by washing wounds, by bringing to life a barren desert and by becoming the focal point of our activities.[4]

Within the realm of the man-made environment, water removes itself from the speculative realm and becomes both sensual and economic. It becomes a representative and structuring element. How the beauty of the Alhambra or the logic of Amsterdam reveal themselves however, helps to set the tone for that environment. If water is nothing but flow, the first act of transformation by man defines its character within the man-made world. It can become one of four things: a point, a line, a pool or an edge. As such, it becomes a point of gathering, a source of power, a place of culture and reflection, or a place of limits and imagination. These are the four fundamental characteristics water takes in architecture. The history of its uses is that in which the physical property is either turned into a man-made equivalent or represented. Over the centuries these two alternatives have become completely hidden, so that now water appears only as a senseless simulation of itself. What is needed is a revelation of the uses of water, both economically and as a system of representation .

The point, first of all, is obviously the spring, welling up from the ground and celebrated in the jets that spout up in the middle of most fountains, and the mysterious grottoes at the top of the Tivoli gardens or in the recesses of Versailles. The spring has magical connotations, which set it aside from the everyday. It is the centre of activity, around which a group can organize itself. In Sforzinda the ideal city of Filarete's, designed in 1497, it is the centre of a Utopia.[5] It is associated with the marketplace and where the community gathers. In its man-made version the spring is the well around which the village groups or, in ancient Rome, the aqueduct spout around which the neighbourhood organises itself. Even in the misogynous world of ancient Greece, the well was the one place where women could gather and create a society.[6] It is perhaps no coincidence that we speak of 'the wellspring of democracy'. Though one can try to control a spring or source, it is difficult, and so it only makes sense as the source for communal activity. It engenders a centralised, radial and communal built form; walls of housing around a common market place with a well, or rooms grouped around a courtyard with a well.

The line is the river, whether the Euphrates, Nile or Rhine. It runs through the landscape and has to be controlled, dammed and parcelled out. It often gives birth to hierarchical societies whose rulers mimic that line in great axes leading not to the water, but to pylons and pyramids that attempt to create order and finitude against the flow of water and life. River cultures are associated with territorialisation, the creation of rigid structures and language, thus replacing nature with an artificial culture. They are the main lines of despotism, against the points of coherence that connect nomadic cultures.[7] In fountains, they are the lines of hierarchy that emanate from the palace of the Cardinal d'Este, the chateau of Fouquet at Vaux-le-Vicomte and the bedroom of Louis XIV at Versailles.[8] Only along this axis does everything make sense.

The pool and the edge mirror each other. The edge is the coast, the delta where earth, water and sky mix and give birth to civilization. Out of the labyrinth waterways of the delta come grids of irrigation. Within this realm one is completely contained with no escape possible. By the 17th century, the Dutch had mirrored this motion of complete containment in their cityscapes and interiors in which all was caught, controlled and at rest. Yet the edge is also the place where another world begins, a place of both danger and possibility. The waterfront is the place where morality breaks down, culture devolves into its own satire and unknown journeys begin. The docks are the places where prostitution flourishes, alcohol clouds the mind and where goods are neither made nor used, but stored, as if they are as much in limbo as the morality of the quay's denizens. Beyond this world of vice and potential there is escape, the floating world crisscrossed by the Ship of Fools, where the relationship between the certainties of architecture and the possibilities of water is reversed. Foucault pointed out that ships, travelling from port to port, that keep society alive: perfect heterotopias, they collage together fragments of cultures across the globe.[9]

In fountains, the edge is the lip or rim that borders the pool. It is the point where distinctions disappear, at the very edge of the place in which the surrounding world is perfectly captured. The pool is a mirror of society, a place where we, like Narcissus, can admire ourselves and where the real and the unreal mix. It represents the very edge of possibilities, since it is both a man-made artifact and something that cannot be contained by man. The pool is where architecture becomes a mirror, a frame that does not contains the possibility of a perfect world, but reflects the world all around us. It presents us back to ourselves. We can only frame water here, and dream by looking in it. Then we can jump in and, like the sailor setting off, enter into another realm of beauty of danger. The edge is the world of Le Lorrain, of the bayou, the setting for Vermeer's reveries, but is also the world of the Salk Institute, of reflecting pools in Washington and the pool paintings of David Hockney.

OPPOSITE: William Pye, Aventino, Mercury House, London; FROM ABOVE: William Pye, Arethusa, Unicorn House, London; Steven Ehrlich, Miller Residence, Los Angeles; Ricardo Legorreta, Solana, Texas

This is a romantic interpretation of the uses of architecture. It assumes that anyone who comes upon a pool, a rivulet, a jet of water or a cascade will understand the complex relationship between the economic needs for water and its systems of representation. We should not be able to look at the waterworks of the Alhambra without understanding this as the site where wave after wave of nomadic cultures settled down, irrigated the land and built a civilisation that so surrounded them that they could only dream of escaping while drowning in its luxuries.

Yet these are only images and speculative connections. In a pragmatic sense, these days water works to enliven architecture. It is a meeting point, whether in the middle of Rome or on the campus of UC Berkeley. The fountain is a place to take children and amuse them. We stroll through water gardens to be delighted and cooled, and maybe to receive a slight sense of the *frisson* that comes from observing the Niagara, the flooding Mississippi or Turner's unconfined seas. Water, the final embellishment of architecture, has become as much a consumable luxury.

The history of water in architecture is, after all, one of suppression. The spring in the oasis becomes a bricked up, enclosed source, often at the heart of a temple or a place of production. From something that wells up in the ground, it becomes hidden, something that only a few have access to. In architecture, the point becomes a jet or *berceau*, often placed inaccessibly in the middle of a basin. In current fountain design, there is often no one point from which water emanates: the firm WET has made it their trademark to create multiple jets that are hidden and surprise the viewer as they shoot up. Instead of mystery, we have a democracy of availability that eludes our grasp.

The line has equally become hidden through history. As soon as we created dikes to control rivers, we took the river from view. Even later, the river became first an aqueduct impervious to the vicissitudes of landscape as it brought its water to some far-off site, and then a sewer running underground. In fountains, the line became a narrow little rivulet that often seemed to defy gravity or, as in Cordoba, performs its function of watering the trees in such a complex pattern that you do not notice the base activity. Where there is a long line, it is either manipulated to tell a story, as in Tivoli, and thus hidden in arbitrary places, or it broadens to become the reflective pools of the Baroque.

The swamp becomes, as I noted above, a grid that transforms the labyrinth into an emblem of clarity, while hemming it in with built form to the point that the notions of travel, commerce and agriculture are all hidden below the grid of the city. More recently, the romance of the dock has been exorcised from the city and removed to the industrial realm of the container port, sanitising both city and edge. The pool, no longer located in small-scale courtyards or in the middle of cities, becomes a reflecting surface that mirrors nothing but the sky, fulfilling the same function in the city as the empty canvas does in art: it represents the unrepresentable within a safely neutral border.

If the 18th century turned water into an illustrative element, the 19th put water to work. For Schinkel[10], the Spree became a staging ground for civic monuments. The river provided the scenographic coherence that had been discovered in such great English gardens as Stourhead, where there was a story of discovery lurking underneath the phenomenal connections. Schinkel, used the twists and turns of the river to place and mirror architecture without providing any power of their own. To Otto Wagner, rivers became the excuse for creating an architecture that illustrated the very logic of the modern state as it regulated and framed the source of movement and drinking water. Whilst to Bertram Goodhue, a river was something that could be turned in its course to serve the creation of the City Beautiful[11], while its real workings were concealed underground.

Ultimately, water is hidden in our society. It exists in sewers, tunnels and water storage tanks that now no longer even loom over rooftops, but hide inside attics or anonymous buildings. When we go to see it, we make trips to dams, the coast, and aquariums. Cities no longer grow around rivers, cataracts, springs, pools and ports, but around airports or highways, in amorphous patterns that defy the presence of water and yet demand it all the same.[12] We often forget how fundamental the vast systems of extraction, purification, distribution and drainage are to our urban life, yet there is little or no trace of them in our man-made environment.

If the gardens of the Alhambra and the canals of Amsterdam represent one model of how both the reality of water and its sensual properties can be represented then we seem now to rely only on the other. This is a baroque method of representation, which collects water into a machine of concentrated picturing that replaces an intrinsic connection with a wholly separate, idealised story. Bernini's great fountain in Rome represents four mythic rivers, none of them anywhere nearby. The water garden in Fort Worth, Texas, creates a man-made waterfall hundreds of miles from the nearest real one. In the Solana Development of Westlake, by Legorreta, the troughs, wells and pools of the desert Southwest provide a romantic aura to a Midwestern office park.

OPPOSITE: Shoei Yoh, Prospecta '92, Toyama

13

This mechanisation of architecture exactly mirrors the rationalisation of water usage. Technology makes the true nature of things invisible, and then recreates it in such a way that it can be controlled, distributed, and turned on and off at will. Our only escape is ritual reconnection through travel; we turn off the autobahn to wander along the Rhine or take our clothes off in the pristine pools of Hawaii. Only in city parks, whether Central Park in New York, with its reservoir that has become a jogging track and its pool reflecting the skyscrapers that becomes a skating rink, or in the Englisher Garten in Munich, where the Aare has become a strip that connects beer gardens to nude beaches to the civic heart of the town, do we still capture the traditional power of aquatic architecture. Perhaps the most poignant attempt to continue the narrative tradition of architecture is the Parc de la Villette, where an industrial canal becomes the site for a line of gun emplacements defending the pseudo Utopia of the park. The central portion is a sunken grotto where you return not to the source, but to the retaining wall that holds, the water back, and the water and sewage pipes do not erupt into expressive fountains, but zoom overhead to unknown destinations like the highways of the modern metropolis.

Which is not to say that we can't still have fun. Certainly Charles Moore helped keep alive the sense of wonder in his Piazza d'Italia and Wonderwall, both in New Orleans. In a more powerful way, the Disney Corporation[13] has turned the swamps of Florida into a water-based park where reality is replaced by its sanitised cousin. In the Wilderness Lodge, a fountain inside the hotel lobby becomes a stream in the High Sierras, tumbles over a waterfall worthy of Tivoli, becomes a swimming pool and hot tub, erupts into a replica of Old Faithful and finally seeps into the swamp, now recast as a great boating lake. Water has become the ultimate show, the thing that makes you believe that anything is possible.

How then can we again find the clarity and wellspring of revelation that would seem to be the essence of water The architect Bill Morrish[14] offered one alternative. He pointed out that the city of Los Angeles exists only by virtue of massive water projects that pipe water into the area from three sources each several hundred miles removed; the Sacramento delta, Owens Valley and the Colorado River. The economics involved with this work has shaped the geography and power structure of the city, as anyone who has viewed Chinatown will know. Yet there are few places where this is evident. The great monuments to the watering of Los Angeles are the Hoover Dam in Nevada, the narrow lines of water that course through the desert and the

giant pipes that course under the ground. All you see is the tap, sink or shower. Even those public fountains that do exist are based on standard models and give little explanation about their source.

Morrish suggested revelations of water in two scales: public monuments, that in their design would pay tribute to the sources of the water and become the focal points for the large-scale public parks Los Angeles[15] today lacks, and mass-produced taps. This innovative project had the one drawback that it fell back again on narrative techniques to expose the true nature of a substance that we take for granted; replacing a true sense of community with a consumer version thereof.[16]

In fact, we have no desire to know where our water comes from, since it would only induce a massive amount of guilt, given the environmental absurdity of the activity of removing such massive amounts of it from one place to another. We do not need public parks when we have not only Disneyland, but also the private pools and public waterparks that give us a controlled version of that sense of community,

The landscape designer Achva Stein[17] has suggested instead that we put unused lots in Los Angeles to use for small scale, drip-agriculture. Rather than planning ever more and more coherent built environments, she suggests that we should leave the decaying urban cores as open land, and make us of the agricultural skills of Los Angeles' large immigrant community to create a new hybrid between city and country. This is, or course, already happening in the exurbs, or Edge Cities, in a completely privatised manner. She proposes instead that we create communities based on urban craft and agriculture that can grow as a kind of tactical *bricolage*. I would suggest that the natural forms for connecting, and representing such growths would be water; the irrigation lines, ditches, collecting pools, sluices and the dams would all form the armature for a new kind of post-urbanism.

The architects Hodgetts & Fung, working with landscape architect Mark Rios and several other collaborators, explored such an expression in their project for a Los Angeles Arts Park. Located in one of the great catch basins that safeguard Los Angeles from the periodic floods to which it is so prone. The project represented that ephemeral, yet threatening presence as a classic, picturesque lake. Whilst, at the same time, the rest of the area was to be covered with the orange groves that gave Los Angeles its first Utopian image. Their irrigation lines above ground and forming the markers through which one would navigate the project. The art of the park was the revelation of water.

The diametric opposite of this approach is

Steven Holl, Stretto House, Texas

James Turrell's 1993 project in Nancy. There, a former public swimming pool became one of the artist's 'sky rooms.' Wearing a special issue bathing suit, you dived underwater, rising up into a room whose floor was water and whose roof was the sky itself. A knife edge border to the ceiling made all sense of enclosure disappear. In this floating world, aquatic architecture finally emerged. Instead of containing water, using it to make money or tell stories, water and sky become interchangeable elements in an architecture that no longer mediates or separates, but merely recomposes all dimensions of your phenomenal reality.

Such are the two Utopian dreams for a true water architecture. Neither the fertile field nor the total swimming pool may be as elegant as the Alhambra, but they have the virtue of being as real and changeable as water itself. In the meantime, we are all caught in the Office of Metropolitan Architecture's Floating Swimming Pool. Constructed by fleeing Soviet students, it traverses the Atlantic by the force of regulated swimming. The pool is a fragment of an architecture that contains, purifies, and converts water into pleasure, a moving ritual and a heterotopic tanker of bureaucracy. Lost in the ocean that covers two thirds of the earth, the Floating Pool is the essence of modern architecture, a structure floating in a sea of desire.

Notes

The most recent general texts on the subject are: Charles Moore, *Water and Architecture*, Harry N Abrams Inc, New York, 1993; Anthony Wilson, *Aquatecture: Architecture and Water*, Architectural Association Press, London, 1986; Craig S Campbell, *Water in Landscape Architecture*, Van Nostrand Reinhold Company, New York, 1978.

1 Cf Ed Taverne, *In't Land van Belofte: In de Nieue Stadt, Ideal en Werkelijkheid van de Stadsuitleg in de Republiek, 1580-1680*, Uitgeverij, Maarsse, 1978; Gary Schwartz, *Opokomst en Bloei van het Noordner-derlandse Stadsgezicht in the 17 de Eeuw*, Londshoff, Amsterdam, 1977.

2 Sveltlana Alpers, *The Art of Describing: Dutch Art in the Seventeenth Century*, University of Chicago Press, Chicago, 1983; Sveltlana Alpers, 'Seeing as Knowing: A Dutch Connection', *Humanities in Society 1*, pp 147-173.

3 For the architectural context of the saltworks, Anthony Vidler, *The Writings of the Wall: Architectural Theory In the Late Enlightenment*, Princeton Architectural Press, New York, 1987; for the general question of the narrative qualities of architecture, Silvia Lavin, *Quatremère de Quincy and the Invention of a Modern Language of Architecture*, MIT press, Cambridge MA, 1993.

4 Moore, ibid, pp 36.

5 For the most interesting and sensual use of water as part of a Utopian Scheme, Aiberto Perez-Gomez, 'Hypnerotomachia Poliphili', *Polyphilo - The Dark Forest Revisited: An Erotic Epiphany of Architecture*, MIT press, Cambridge MA, 1993.

6 Cf Eva C Keuls, *The Reign of the Phallus: Sexual Politics in Ancient Athens*, Harper and Row, New York, 1985.

7 This interpretation of the emergence of an absolute architecture is grounded in Lewis Mumford, *The City in History: Its Origins, Its Transformations and Its Prospects*, Harcourt Brace Yovanovich, New York, 1989 (1961), but also draws on Deleuze and Félix Guattari,

A Thousand Plateaux, translation by Brian Massumi, University of Minnesota Press, Minneapolis, 1987; Bruce Chatwins, *The Song-lines*, Vintage Books, New York, 1987, presents a similar argument in a more sweeping and literary manner through a close examination of the world of the Australian Aborigines.

8 For the best summary description and interpretation of Vaux-le-Vicomte, Vincent Scully, *Architecture: the Natural and the Man-made*, St Martin's Press, New York, 1991, pp 237-265.

9 Michel Foucault, 'Other Spaces. The principles of Heterotopia', *Lotus 48/49*, 1986, pp 10-24.

10 Kurt Forster, 'Schinkel in Berlin', lectures at the Southern California Institute of Architecture, Los Angeles, March-April, 1985.

11 Cf William H Wilson, *The City Beautiful Movement*, John Hopkins University Press, Baltimore, 1989.

12 One could argue that cities now grow in ways that Deleuse and Guattari might call rhizomatic, rather than depending for their source of water on centralised root systems.

13 The Disney corporation has collected the fullest range of examples of the uses of water in architecture at their Orlando, Florida Disneyworld. Built on a swamp this theme park has fountains, pools, canals, lakes, waterfalls and even pseudo-underwater experiences.

14 William Morrish, 'Urban Spring: Formalising the Water System of Los Angeles', *Modulus 17*, 1984, pp 45-73.

15 Cf Marc Reisner, *Cadillac Desert: The American West and its Disappearing Water*, Penguin Books, New York, 1987; Margaret Lesile Davis, *Rivers in the Desert: William Mulholland and the Inventing of Los Angeles*, Harper Collins, New York, 1993.

16 Rem Koolhaas, *Delirious New York: A Retroactive Manifesto for Manhattan*, George Brazillier, New York, 1978.

17 Achva Stein, conversations with the Author, Spring, 1994.

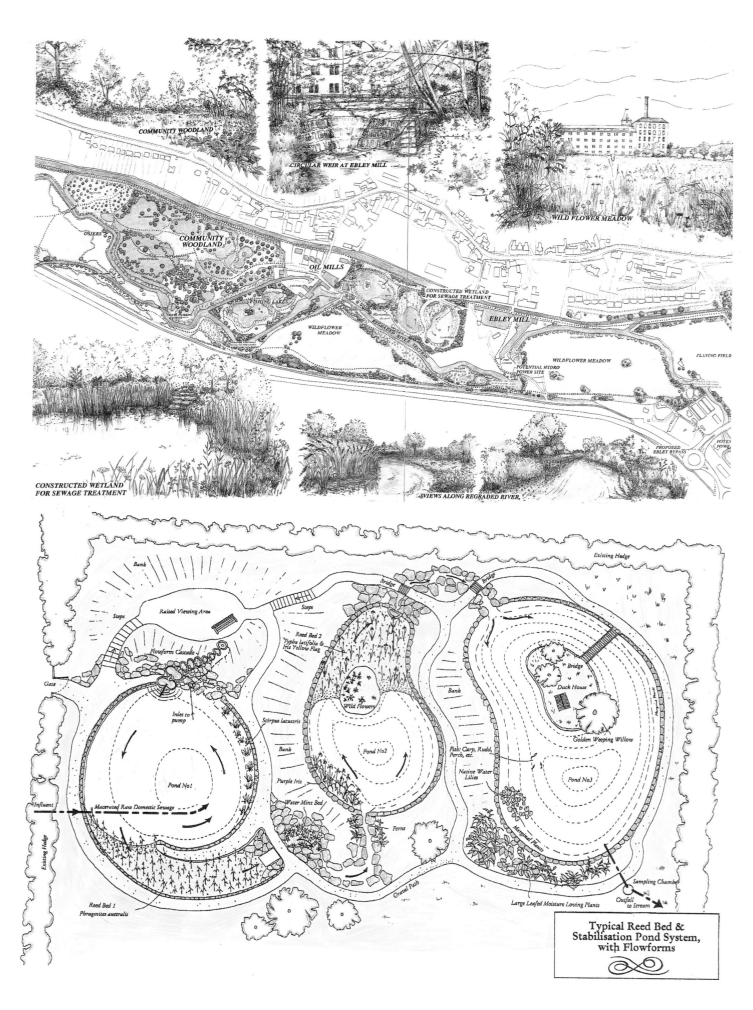

COMMUNITY WOODLAND

CIRCULAR WEIR AT EBLEY MILL

WILD FLOWER MEADOW

OSIERS

COMMUNITY WOODLAND

OIL MILLS

CONSTRUCTED WETLAND FOR SEWAGE TREATMENT

FISHING LAKES

WILDFLOWER MEADOW

EBLEY MILL

WILDFLOWER MEADOW

PLAYING FIELD

POTENTIAL HYDRO POWER SITE

PROPOSED EBLEY BYPASS

POTEN POWE

CONSTRUCTED WETLAND FOR SEWAGE TREATMENT

VIEWS ALONG REGRADED RIVER

Existing Hedge

Bank

Raised Viewing Area

Steps

Steps

Bridge

Bridge

Reed Bed 2
Typha latifolia & Iris Yellow Flag

Bridge

Duck House

Flowform Cascade

Gate

Inlet to pump

Scirpus lacustris

Wild Flowers

Bank

Golden Weeping Willow

Existing Hedge

Pond No1

Bank

Purple Iris

Pond No2

Fish: Carp, Rudd, Perch, etc.

Native Water Lilies

Pond No3

Influent

Macerated Raw Domestic Sewage

Water Mint Bed

Ferns

Reed Bed 1
Phragmites australis

Gravel Path

Large Leafed Moisture Loving Plants

Marginal Plants

Sampling Chamber

Outfall to Stream

Typical Reed Bed & Stabilisation Pond System, with Flowforms

JULIAN JONES
WATER – DESIGNING FOR PLENTY AND PURITY

I f there is any single most important factor limiting human development on our planet, then it must surely be problems with water quality and quantity. Certainly in Britain, and most other developed countries, good water availability has long been taken for granted, even though until recently it was one of the daily list of essentials to worry about. The Victorian era, with its great municipal sanitation and water supply schemes did so much to banish these problems. Yet curiously now, more than a century later, all is not so rosy in the garden.

While Malthusian[1] enthusiasts might claim there are now some serious signs of strain in the 'system', our nations and their economies still lumber on, from one crisis to the next; aware that the danger of atomic doom, whether real or imagined, has now been replaced by the threat of planetary environmental catastrophe. Just as with the old left-right political polarity, you will be on one side of the environmental fence or the other in perceiving the relevance of these matters.

However, water is different. The problems here are not only fundamental to life, they are undeniably real and quantifiable. They also provide a finite focus, at least causing inconvenience and at the worst death, through thirst, disease and drowning. These aspects are increasingly making themselves felt in the prosperous West, through their daily coverage on the news: water usage restrictions applied from California to Kent; 400,000 people infected with Cryptosporidium[2] in just one incident in the US Mid-West; serious flooding on the Rhine and Mississippi; and record sales of bottled water. Considering we live on the so-called 'Water Planet', surely we should have mastered this aspect of our lives by now.

It seems safe to assume that ever more expensive water charges are a valid indication that we have been getting it very wrong, and that actually a complete rethink is now needed. However, this appears to be slowly getting under way: a mild and gentle revolution in the light of changing public perceptions and increased consciousness of the environment.

This all appears to be symptomatic of our society's 'detachment from nature', and as we might expect water, the planetary lifeblood, is a good indicator of any problems in our interaction here. Should this really be the case then it will have major implications for almost every aspect of the built environment. The resolution of these issues will require that architects are even more aware of them and expand their working briefs accordingly.

Environmental audits, and impact studies, should take the widest possible view; considering the total impact both on and from local water resources, as well as their availability. It even appears unwise to rely on water utilities these days, as to do so can create future problems, restrictions and escalating charges. Besides there are alternatives that will prove cheaper in the long run, as well as benefiting the immediate and wider community. Considering this, it is not all doom and gloom. Far from it in fact, as out of problems come opportunities, and forward thinking never does any harm.

There is now the tantalising prospect that, whether you are a hose banned gardener in Kent you should have been saving that bath water, or an Ogadeni nomad at their last gasp, shouldn't have chopped down those trees. The new consciousness associated with these problems will ultimately prove to be a great global leveller and educator, leading to the justification that ecological engineering, working closely with natural principles, will provide the thread with which to darn our frayed ecosphere. Certainly, it can generate a universally understood language of design criteria as the basic principles of natural water management are the same the world over. If we can get our water management 'correct', then it will help so much else fall into place.

'Water prophets' date back to Noah and much New Age thinking on water has a biblical feel to it. The great modern seer who set off the current phase of thinking was probably the rather mythical Victor Schauberger.[3] Born in 1885, he spent his youth in the forests of Austria observing the natural processes and phenomena, particularly the magical role of water in an otherwise undisturbed environment.

Water is of course a rather special substance, defying conventional laws of physics; it expands 11% when cooled to freezing, but weighs most at precisely four degrees centigrade, the reason that ice floats. Although not

Stroud Urban Wetlands: natural sewage treatment for 4,000 people

17

an anomaly, it is also worth noting that the latent heat capacity of water is most favourable at thirty-seven degrees centigrade, human body temperature. The interaction of water within the environment and our own bodies, relies upon these, and further subtle properties, that we are only now beginning to grasp. It seems incredible that 'heretics' such as Schauberger tried to warn us of this nearly a century ago. As *Hoechst High Chem Magazine* [4] put it in December 1992, 'Only now is modern science unravelling, step by step, the mysteries of water's global circulation and its many consequences for life on Earth'. A worrying admission from the scientists, in whom we have entrusted our faith.

We can all observe the undisturbed, natural passages of water across a landscape, as well as our ultimately futile attempts to control them. After decades of river management boards trying to straighten rivers out, based on the flawed premise that this would help the control of flood water, there is now a growing appreciation of the meanders' value. Their form is a mathematical function of the water volume, soil substrata and gradient, engineered by the action of the vortices of flow which traverse, in a twin corkscrew effect, across a stream, as an aspect of the downstream current. The river itself is just a minor component within a larger system of tributaries, wetlands and forests, essential for the cleansing and storage of water. As Schauberger stated:

> We must understand how Mother Nature transforms water into the lifeblood of the planet and makes it available to us, pure and life giving. If we succeed in this quest there would be no reason why this earth could not be transformed into a garden, supplying an unimaginable and delectable harvest.

An intriguing concept from a man whose work with the forms and shapes used by nature led him to startling conclusions in the field of benign energy production.

In 1961, Theodore Schwenk a former hydrological engineer, published *Sensitive Chaos*, exploring man's changing relationship to water. The text notes it being taken for granted and our abdication of responsibility for its well being. In an earlier age, Herodotus made the extreme suggestion that we should not even wash in rivers.

Schwenk observed our habits of clearing forests, draining wetlands and straightening rivers and felt that these practices were disturbing the whole delicate organism of nature itself. That not only were we going to cause the type of problems we are now seeing but, even more disturbingly, we were tampering with the actual source of life itself. Admittedly this is a highly esoteric perception of the function of

water, and certainly too insubstantial for many. However, for others it is a view that will pose the question of just how deep our understanding and integration with nature needs to be, and how this knowledge can be applied.

The thought that we might in some way be compromising water's life sustaining abilities would ring true to any believers in homoeopathy. They believe that water retains a 'memory' of active ingredients, long after they have been diluted well beyond any actual physical presence. Such ideas, if valid, raise the possibility of water carrying all sorts of bad 'memories' as a result of our mismanagement. Also, consider what might be the deleterious effects of pumping and straight pipes. If concepts such as these sound absurd now, remember that to many the importance of wetlands and even rain forests seemed the same not 80 years ago.

Schwenk, like Schauberger, noted the propensity of water to form vortices and the prevalence of the spiral form throughout nature. Yet no one has applied these principles to our day-to-day uses of water, as pigs-tail piping and pulsating pumps, though apparently not so daft, are hardly practical. Is any of this really relevant, does it really matter that our rivers are now for much of the time so short of water and misshapen that they lose their vortical flows?

The search for a simple method of restoring this quality to water was picked up by the artist and sculptor John Wilkes in 1962. Whilst the original purpose of Wilkes' quest may remain unproved, the peripheral fruits of this work are ready for consumption and can answer many of the common aquatic problems with which we are now all too well aware. By 1970 Wilkes had developed sequences of organic, vertebra like shapes, called Flowforms, within which the streaming water adopted a pulsating, rhythmical, figure of eight flow path.

In 1973, Wilkes collaborated with Arne Klingborg, exploring the Flowform as an 'organ' of regeneration, within a larger 'organism' for the cleansing of sewage and waste water. Together, they create beautiful water gardens at the Rudolf Steiner School, Järna, Sweden, for just this purpose. It is time for a radical rethink on the 'flush and forget' mentality and to produce a statement of environmental responsibility that accords entirely with Steiner's theories of 'Anthroposophy'.

Flowforms also have other applications. The NMB Bank, Amsterdam, an example of *Baubiologie* building, has numerous Flowforms incorporated into its design, some running down the handrails of stairs. Quite apart from their ornamental value they are effective at cooling interior spaces, and when combined with plants provide natural air conditioning. It should be noted that a marked decline in staff

Wenk Associates, Shop Creek, Aurora, Colorado

sickness was observed at the bank after the introduction of Flowforms.

At Järna a series of seven ponds, with beds of gravel, planted with varieties of aquatic plants and interspersed with Flowform cascades still provides effective cleansing for 200 persons, 20 years after its construction. Some of Wilkes' students have gone on to develop these reed bed techniques further, combining them with the findings of other independent researchers, notably Kathe Seidal. Such work now stands in the vanguard of potential alternative aquatic solutions.

'Making water work' was a slogan used to promote the recent privatisation of the water industry in England and Wales. The whole process caused great public unease then and now, five years on, there are serious doubts whether it is indeed 'working' and meeting ever growing public expectations for high environmental standards at a reasonable cost.

Privatisation is generally held to be a means of ensuring competition and improving efficiency. However, in the case of water a different reason was tendered, it was 'to enable the large investments required', for as it was a monopoly there could be no competition. Nevertheless, if competition is now allowed with telephones, electricity and shortly gas, why not water? There is no engineering reason to prevent competition and there are many economic and health reasons to encourage it. Reed bed sewage treatment is far superior to centralised sewerage monopolies, and architects are well placed to advise developers of this option, as an environmentally responsible component of any development.

The term 'sewage farm' arose from the practice of grass-plot treatment of sewage onto farmland, a practice largely discontinued as chemical process engineers took over the treatment of sewage. It is now apparent that they were the wrong people for the job. In terms of a cost and benefit analysis nature can be proven to be the finest and cheapest water engineer, using either reed beds or constructed wetlands. These are superefficient grass-plots whose construction costs are typically only half those of conventional sewage treatment works, with running costs of only ten percent. Even these financial benefits are only part of the picture, also there are secondary benefits that make the case for such natural water management overwhelming.

The principles of hydro-botanic uptake of nutrients, the major component of sewage, has been understood since at least 1699, when an Englishman, John Woodward discovered hydroponics. However, there are apocryphal claims that the Hanging Gardens of Babylon were an early attempt at municipal sanitation.

Looking much like a series of paddy field terraces and ponds, the main cleansing process within RBT is the microbial activity, both bacterial and algal. This is an aerobic/anoxic process, as oxygen is pumped down through their roots or rhizomes, as opposed to the anaerobic, or septic type, which is responsible for the malodours often linked with sewage treatment. Further cleansing takes place from enzyme activity associated with the various plants and also the simple sedimentation and filtration effects in the gravel bed and pond construction. A variety of flow regimes are encouraged including submerged, horizontal flow beds, and free draining, vertical flow beds and lagoons, or stabilisation ponds. These take up between two and eleven metres squared per person and are grouped according to site topography and effluent type, which allows industrial waste to be dealt with. Design parameters are simple enough, but expert assistance should be sought until experience is gained. Thereafter, it is a job for architects, with farmers and local authorities owning and operating those on a municipal scale.

A former student of John Wilkes', Andrew Joiner, of Iris Water, has refined the technology to the point of mimicking the tidal conditions found in estuaries, through the use of automatic siphons between stages. This system has been implemented at the Trossachs Hotel in Scotland and serves over 600 people.

Flowform sculpture can be justified for its gentle aeration benefits alone, but the aesthetic properties are also appreciated by many. The rhythm generated can be observed in natural settings to boost the growth of microbes. These are encouraged in the controlled setting of a reed bed, and the diversity of the system makes it more resilient to shock overloads than conventional treatment.

At one time 50% of the UK land area comprised wetlands. According to The Wildfowl & Wetland Trust, Slimbridge the total is now less than two per cent, much of this due to agricultural drainage and flood plain development. This is repeated all over the world and it is now time to start restoring wetlands, as they are 'nature's kidneys' cleaning and storing water. Grants are now available to farmers in Europe for this, and the Dutch government is actually planning, after centuries of creating land, to return 15% to wetland, assisting with flood control on the Rhine. Wetlands, natural and constructed, can also fulfil a wide range of other vital functions in addition to flood relief, providing buffering for excess rainfall, water storage, the supply of resources, conservation areas and leisure activities.

Reed bed treatment appears to be the vanguard of a sustainable lifestyle for our

FROM ABOVE: Shamrock Flowform, Trossachs Hotel, Scotland; detail of Shamrock Flowform, Trossachs Hotel, Scotland; Mälmo Flowform cascade, Trossachs Hotel, Scotland

society. The thin end of a very thick wedge of 'green' alternatives with major benefits for continuing food and energy production. Proving the benefit of all these so-called alternatives becomes much easier when viewing the full picture and understanding the interrelationships between its parts. The holistic view is essential here. RBT helps farming by returning non toxic humus to the land, which aids water retention and storage, which in turn helps to even out river flows. This is quite alien to the water industry, through no sinister reason, other than it is made up of groups of highly qualified specialists, each with only a narrow view of the overall picture.

Public care for the environment is the greatest engine for change now. Last summer water rate payers burnt their bills on the streets of south west England. This was not just due to ever increasing charges but also heightening environmental awareness. The reality is that the plans for the privatisation of UK water were based on unsustainable and outdated concepts dating back to the Victorian Era. While environmentalist concern was a minority interest a decade ago its popularity is now increasing.

Farm fertilisation with sewage is problematic, as the direct return of human waste to our food chain may be dangerous. The commonest problem with sewage fertilisation is the accumulation of heavy metals in the sludge. These are derived from industrial waste, which a centralised sewerage system conveniently dilutes and neutralises with domestic sewage. Reed beds again benefit here by allowing *in situ* treatment to decentralise the system, segregating the two waste types. One industry's waste can be another's raw material. However, there are other benefits as localised treatment cuts pumping and trunk sewer costs by returning water straight back to rivers, rather than short-circuiting the hydrological cycle.

Decentralisation of sewerage is now crucial for health reasons, as it is only recently that we have appreciated the long life of sewage viruses in the sea; upwards of a year. Despite the extensive catalogue of accepted potential risks to health from direct contact with sewage, successive governments have allowed the practice of discharging raw, or macerated sewage into the sea, within the legal limits. These acceptable levels of risk are unbelievably based on a 1959 study which concluded that bathing in sewage polluted sea water carried only a negligible risk to health, and a further study, in 1974, that found that 'microbial standards for bathing water are irrelevant to the public health'. Also, two other factors have exacerbated this situation: the lack of past public interest and also the erroneous belief that high costs were involved in rectifying any

problems. All three of these key determinants are now no longer valid.

When we apply this new knowledge, of health risks, to the situation of rivers at present we should be alarmed. In the UK alone, there are some 30,000 'storm' overflows and these are regularly used when sewers collapse or block up. Without the necessary dilution and cleansing action of rainwater waste material can build up, posing a direct risk not only to paddling children but also from breathing in minuscule water droplets. This spray is generated at weirs, when rain finally washes away the waste, and can travel for miles. Far smaller volumes of aerosols escaping from air-conditioning systems have in the past been responsible for legionnaire's disease.

Thus we can now see the Victorian ideal of monolithic, centralised municipal water and sewage systems, once thought to be the epitome of good sanitation practice, now contribute to low water levels in rivers and as they progressively collapse through old age are actively distributing pathogens into our environment: either through storm overflows, or via cross-contamination from damaged sewers to adjacent leaky mains, a documented phenomenon and incidentally the reason for high chlorination levels in tap water.

We cannot simply do away with these sewers and overflows, as long as storm water is allowed into municipal sewerage systems but, there must be facilities for safely letting it out again. There is, of course, a further type of reed bed design that can be used to strain any overflow waste but, this is only a short term solution. In the longer term, rather than trying to get rainwater out to sea as quickly as possible, ways should be examined that can keep it inland, returning it to the water cycle. Infiltration basins, returning it to ground water are one possibility, whilst more trees and increased ground vegetation are another.

Small scale freshwater storage is viable, cheap and environmentally preferable to mains and pumping stations, and also saves energy. The water industry reasons for not fully using reed beds have ranged from 'not enough space' to 'third world technology'. As Severn Trent Water put it after a recent visit to the Britain from an Eastern European delegation, reed beds are 'cheap, simple and effective – ideal for Poland'. So, why not here, as this is globally relevant technology. The reason is because of the perpetuation of the myth that sewerage infrastructure needs be so expensive. After years of telling the public that charges have to go up, who would dare say they could be halved? Farmers maybe, as they have the land to spare, even in urban fringe areas, and the skills.

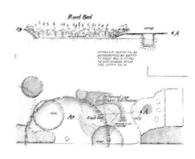

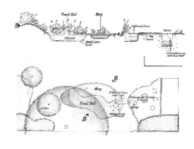

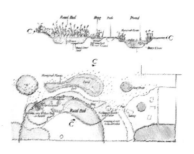

FROM ABOVE: Basic, unlined reed bed for polishing septic tank effluent; lined reed bed for cleansing septic tank effluent; typical reed bed and stabilisation pond system with flowforms

However, the Water Acts do allow for competition in certain circumstances. At present levels a reed bed would return up to £25,000 pa/ha income for a farmer, which certainly beats set aside, and no doubt there would be some room for negotiation. It is all a question of attitude: would not every street like its own water garden? How about if it cut water bills in half, and through providing high quality recycled water, negated the need for water metering? Some planning authorities already allow for reed bed treatments in local structure plans.

Public awareness is awakening from a long slumber. Perhaps we have realised that William Blake was right when he predicted that 'All the Arts of Life . . .' would become 'the Arts of Death in Albion', owing to our blindness to 'the simple rules of life' and we would spend our days in 'sorrowful drudgery'. Blake predicted this in the same piece that he prophesied the destruction of the water wheels. Now we can draw a direct parallel between the water wheel and the modern hydro-turbine. There are over 15,000 such viable sites in the Britain, that could supply over ten per cent of our electricity and also clean our rivers, straining out rubbish and providing aeration. We don't use them because the accountants would advise against it. Hydro-turbine typically take five years to cover capital costs against the two years for a gas turbine, this overlooks that the hydro turbine would still be producing truly free electricity in 50 years.

Perhaps reed beds are just too simple. Was it our search for technology or our greed that blinded us? It was the Victorian era that heralded the 'flush it and forget it' mentality and the engineering for this, which seemed to work during this period of reduced consciousness but now we know otherwise.

The saving grace of the whole UK water privatisation process is the vaunted, though still yet to be properly applied, free market. We are the arbiters of the marketplace through our purchasing decisions, that allows us the ultimate expression of public wishes.

Economists would do well to investigate the possibilities and financial implications of ecological engineering. An ancient Greek would have recognised the primacy of *Logos* (the formative principle of something; in ancient eyes, the divine mind that animates the world) over *Nomos* (the laws of life deduced from the *Logos*), sadly though for the moment economics still controls the ecologies.

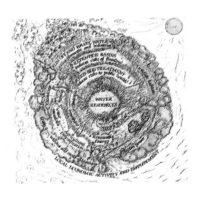

In sewerage and water there is a host of natural technologies that can provide much, for relatively little, whilst also performing the alchemy of creating real wealth out of 'nothing', or otherwise presently wasted resources. These would appear to be sensible steps towards stabilising our otherwise highly artificial and unstable economies. Inflation is a symptom of too much money chasing too few resources. Architects have a key role to play here and it all seems to start with looking after water. After all, this was supposed to be the Age of Aquarius.

Notes

1 After Thomas Malthus, economist and demographer, born Dorking, England Feb 17th, 1766, died Dec 23rd, 1834 Bath. He theorised that population growth would outrun food supply and other resources, stating that for the betterment of mankind reproduction should be controlled.

2 A protozoal parasite commonly found in cattle and pig manures, which is transmissible to humans via polluted water supplies.

3 Austrian naturalist and iconoclast, 1885-1958. He presented a completely new understanding of the potential of natural energy. He warned that modern man was sowing the seeds of his own destruction by working against Nature.

4 Monthly journal of Germany's largest chemical manufacturing company, Hoechst Aktiengesellschaft, D-6320, Frankfurt am Main 80.

FROM ABOVE: Actual sewage works, Stroud Urban Wetlands (cost £1.25 million); natural treatment with superior performance, Stroud Urban Wetlands (cost £0.4 million); the principles of natural water management

CHARLES MOORE
THE POTENTIAL FOR WONDER

Today, when water has become increasingly domesticated and decreasingly appreciated, even a short visit to Bear Run is filled with affirmations of water's indefatigable magic and excitement. The messages are especially potent since many of us have grown accustomed to taking fresh, clean water for granted. Water instantly flows out of our taps, showers and toilets, and most of us give little thought to where the water came from, or where it goes after we pull the plug. Modern treatment plants have replaced the natural water cycle with a mechanised hydrologic cycle of collection, filtration and sedimentation. After the water passes standardised purity tests, it is released into networks of underground pipes and, with the turn of a wrist, fills our waiting glasses.

All of this effort is expended for the simple reason that we need water to live. Undeniably, water has a tangible physical hold on the lives of every one of us. However, water also has many intangible meanings for humans, ranging from birth in the amniotic fluid, to death in the mythical waters of the river Styx. More than anything, designs involving water and architecture must remind people of this dual impact that water has on our lives.

The reminders can be very simple. In ancient Pompeii there was a drinking fountain for people and donkeys. It had a straightforward shape and made water conveniently available for the townspeople and their animals. Above the fountain was a relief depicting a cloud with a rain god on top. For the donkeys, it added nothing of value to the water, but for the women and men who came there to drink, it was a reminder of where the water had come from and how it fitted into their religious and physical scheme of the world. The relief invested the fountain with meaning, communicating something about Pompeian beliefs and attitudes and a reminder that people are not donkeys.

Architects use materials and forms to communicate ideas. When we make places that include water in our designs, we cannot ignore the role that history and symbolism play in fortifying connections among people, water and nature. Perhaps the greatest lesson of our century has been that people need connections to the past, and myths or religions, to help make some sense of our increasingly complex world. If architecture were merely built of materials and composed of empty forms, then fountains, gardens and buildings would mean nothing more to people than did the Pompeii fountain for the donkeys drinking there. Clearly this is not the case. In reality, materials and forms are rich with shared or personal meanings. From the ordering of materials and forms the observer should be able to understand something about the use of the design and the people by, and for whom, it was built.

Wayward turtles, sunken barges, flinching river gods and winged sea horses invest the Roman fountains, Tartarughe, Barcaccia, Four Rivers, and Trevi with a resoundingly human dimension. Their lesson is that people know and love places not only for physical attributes, but also for the colourful tales and legends passed on from generation to generation. What would the water in Venice be without its tradition, or the river in Paris without its history? Stourhead not only reminds us of the ideal people once placed on emulating nature in the pursuit of beauty, but also allows us to step out of our lacklustre shoes and step into the shoes of Aeneas. A similar kind of reverence and enthusiasm for nature invests Japanese and Chinese gardens with a palpable spirit, so that every stone, plant and body of water embodies a particular ideal of nature, accessible to those patient enough to seek it out.

Water is a natural material with an unchanging identity. Its use in architecture should reflect the attitude about the natural world held by the people who design, construct and inhabit the building. Since our own relation to the natural world has superseded the historic Western imposition of a geometric order on nature and the Eastern quest for 'naturalness', our use of water in architectural composition will be related to the more complex geometries of our own day, which operate in time as well as in space. At the end of our millennium, we are faced with the dilemma of balancing human needs with respect for nature. If water is being used neither much nor well in our own architecture, then surely some of the difficulty can be traced to our confusion over what sort of attitude toward nature we are trying to express. Yet if we can effectively incorporate water's

Moore Ruble Yudell, Plaza Las Fuentes, Pasadena

23

symbolism, history and physical nature, then our water and architecture can have a potential for wonder unmatched by any other material that we can include in our environments.

Architecture and water engage us by letting us see, hear and touch the water in a myriad of ways. Sight, sound and contact have characterised the inception of buildings, from mediaeval Chinese gardens to European canal cities to harbours old and new. Architecture is an intermediary that negotiates connections, or separations, between people and water, communicating sensory clues through forms and materials. But what combination of senses makes places successful, so that fountains, pools, rivers, harbours, gardens, islands and streams inspire, amuse, rescue, frighten, or challenge us? What similar clues lead us to understand a city's history, a fountain's meaning or a garden's spirit?

Designers at Giverny, Katsura, San Antonio and even the Piazza di Spagna in Rome, use reflection, dance and stillness to create places where people can escape the ordinary, relieve tired minds, or block out distractions. The success of Monet's pond derives from its surface, which is literally filled with reflection. Gardeners engulfed the banks with irises, flooded the surface with lilies, and created a canopy of branches and vines, all fusing to make Giverny an Edenic microenvironment. Katsura's success depends on landscaping devices that build up the shores with rich counterpoints of shapes, colours and textures to achieve a sense of closure. San Antonio's secret is that the waterway is separated from the city by a winding canyon, lined with inviting restaurants, friendly shops, and intimate theatres. We never see it entirely but have to follow its unfolding course. The river walk disconnects us from the rest of the city and draws us together along an interactive street. Like nearly all fountains, the Barcaccia casts spells on people by its magical manipulation of water. Through a sleight of hand, spewing shells, squirting jets and water sloshing over the decks divert attention away from crazed motorists reeling through the piazza.

Designers also use the qualities of reflection, depth and the seemingly infinite surface of large bodies of water to relieve claustrophobia and expand personal space. Instead of hypnotically drawing us inward, the waters of the Four Rivers Fountain, Shugaku-in, Stourhead, Lower Slaughter and the garden of the Master of the Nets release our spirits, guiding our eyes into the sky, the mesmerizing depths of a pool or spacious landscapes. The charming liquid choreography of the Four Rivers Fountain and the mountain's obelisk capped ascent lift spirits us upward and out of the

crowded city. Water at Stourhead helps to deepen space by pulling the foreground forward and pushing the background back. The pond's edges, so carefully integrated into the landscape, undulate to lengthen the perimeter and make the surface area seem larger than if it were a simple circle or oval. Unlike Giverny's edges, which crowd out views into the French countryside, Shugaku-in incorporates neighbouring mountains and rice fields into its design, so that the garden communicates with the 'authentic' and expansive landscape beyond. If the stream flowing through Lower Slaughter were an asphalt lane, it would undoubtedly lose its magic: asphalt lanes do not call to mind all asphalt lanes in the world. As a connecting waterway, however, its currents carry the imagination beyond the town, through central England, to the infinite ocean. On the other hand, the Master of the Nets, with its liquid courtyard, relieves claustrophobia by creating a negative space that in the middle of crowded Suzhou is refreshingly empty.

Like Suzhou, jam-packed Hong Kong constantly barrages the mind with noises and restless commotion, but along its long edge, the harbour contrasts the city's hyperdensity with a wide-open field of blue that, in spite of the ships and boats, grants us a freeing vision of releasing emptiness. A substantial part of the wonder of the Sea Ranch condominiums is that the embracing courtyards and sheltering interiors break loose, through openings, passageways or windows to the vast expanse of the Pacific. People can choose, according to their needs or moods, to be in a small, intimate space or to stand at the edge of the cliff and connect emotionally with the sea. For scientists cooped up in small laboratories, the court at the Salk Institute must be a welcoming relief. Tired eyes can follow Louis Kahn's narrow channel as it becomes thinner and falls into Shelley's 'unfathomable sea.'

Channels of water are excellent devices for unifying complicated architectural arrangements. Waterways can link a series of incidents or provide an element of continuity within a city, such as Chicago, where skyscrapers, a forest of Wrigleys, Tribunes, Monadnocks and Searses, contrast with the unchanging river and lakeshore. When gardeners release the valves at the Villa d'Este, water races through the fountains like the ball bearings in Japanese Pachinko games and, through its constant downward rush, weaves the garden together. At the Villa Lante, Vignola ingeniously used a liquid spine for his symmetrical arrangement of Renaissance balance and harmony. At both the Villa d'Este and the Villa Lante, we can perceive, though not quite see, the continuous flow of water through several chapters of an unfold-

OPPOSITE: Moore Ruble Yudell, Church of the Nativity, Santa Fe; ABOVE: Moore Ruble Yudell, Plaza Las Fuentes, Pasadena; BELOW: Moore Ruble Yudell, Church of the Nativity, Santa Fe

25

ing saga. In the same vein but on a grander scale, the Nile's water acted as the main transportation artery, the source of essential nutrients and a symbol of Egypt. Parisians do not rely on the Seine to flood Notre Dame or the Latin Quarter, nor is it much used for transportation any more, but it continues to link monuments, parks, bridges and streets into a coherent city and absorb the reflections of the buildings lined up along its banks.

There is something about reflection that stirs the heart. Reflection should be used sparingly when dignifying important buildings, but it can be used generously to make ordinary buildings seem more pleasing. Not every building can, or ought to, be lavished with costly materials, but reflecting water can give a building a little extra something. Even though the majority of vernacular buildings in Venice, Suzhou and Amsterdam are humble, the reflecting water in the canals fills them with a magic that the same type of buildings in drier cities cannot match. Reflective water adds an element of fantasy to architecture by filling shadows with light, transforming the solidity of stone or brick to something more transitory and painting what would otherwise be a grey asphalt road with constantly changing colour.

People marvel at reflections. Narcissus adored his own image in the water, and visitors to the lavishly carved and gilded Byodo-in and Kinkaku-ji contemplate visions of the treasured object as a heavenly mansion. If the reflecting pool at the Taj Mahal were drained and planted with grass, the tomb would lose a great deal of its mystery. Reflective water idealises places we build to symbolise the gods we worship, the heroes we intend to remember or the ideals we cherish. Moreover, the pools clear out an unoccupiable space in front of buildings so that we can view them free of the more mundane components of a city. The water in the Tidal Basin and the Reflecting Pool signals that the Jefferson, Lincoln and Washington monuments are very special and are distinguished from the other monuments, agencies, and landmarks in Washington DC.

Architects can use the flat plane that water naturally seeks as an embellishment for compositions. Like the Egyptian pyramids standing in their sea of sand or the Statue of Liberty rising out of New York harbour, Mont-Saint-Michel is a potent three-dimensional object in its own right, but the two-dimensional sheet of water that surrounds it episodically magnifies the outline and sculptural quality of the stirring image. The magic of the Piazza San Marco in Venice is due in part to the pavement extending into the lagoon as well as the apparent flatness of its surface, which helped to earn its distinction as the 'drawing room' of Europe. We are tricked into thinking the piazza itself is perfectly flat by the linear paving pattern, which establishes the horizontal plane strongly enough so that the darker pavement between the lines can slope unobserved to the drains. In addition to the symbolic notion of tying the most important urban space with the sea, a more physical reality is ushered in when high tide invades the piazza, in minutes creating a lagoon among the buildings. If the Torii threshold were moved to the centre of a city or transplanted to a garden, it would lose virtually all of its mystique. The flat blue plane of the bay sets the image apart, contrasting the gate with a field of changing colour and isolating it from physical approach, forcing us to pass through in our imaginations or occasionally in boats. In the same sense, we cannot get close enough to touch the mythological menagerie in the Trevi but must use our imaginations to connect with the sprays of the *Acqua Vergine* streaming from Oceanus.

Like the purely visual aspects of water, the sounds of water are variable and can be manipulated to produce satisfying results. Water makes sound as it splashes against things, moves over solid objects or falls into itself. Attention to the audible aspects of water is important. Too little sound can be annoying, like a dripping tap, and too much sound in confined spaces, like shopping malls, can be overpowering and trite. Franz Liszt spent time at an apartment in the Villa d'Este and was influenced by the sounds of the fountains when he composed *Les Jeux à la Villa d'Este*. In *La Mer*, Claude Debussy tried to simulate the sounds of the sea, violently stormy in full chords or gently lapping in soft dissonances and consonances. Like his contemporary in Venice, the painter Canaletto, Handel was inspired by the pageantry of water festivals, fireworks and royal processions on the Thames; whilst Vivaldi described scenes from the four seasons through the pizzicato of raindrops, the apprehensive, swaying rhythm of a summer storm and its gusty release, con spirito.

Designs can borrow from natural cycles and sounds already present: Fallingwater is constantly filled with the seasonal stream sounds, while Mont-Saint-Michel is always surrounded by the sounds of the sea. But in the absence of brooks or oceans, designers can use water to simulate sounds that allow people to connect with nature, refresh spent minds or block out less desirable noises. The Lovejoy in Oregon is an unexpected surprise in the centre of tame Portland for its impressive amount of water seemingly out of control. Cascade Charley at the University of Oregon, designed by Alice Wingwall, is a much sought after neighbour at lunchtime for the lively sound of its waters.

Silence, too, is appreciated. Water often

makes no sound at all, or very little, so people find emotional rescue in this rare commodity. Just the right amount of water noise can take the edge off of silence, producing white noise. In the middle of Rome, the Tartarughe Fountain only drips feeble squirts of water but is somehow just loud enough to spark the imagination. At the Alhambra, the fountains are relatively quiet, but the stone cloisters, walls, columns and pavements create enchanting echoes and reverberations of the trickles. Lakes are particularly quiet drawing people to connect with their stillness or, like Goethe and Thoreau, to commune with the 'indwelling spirit,' and the Ryoan-ji garden uses stones to create a world that is utterly soundless.

Water touching our skin is the most personally intimate experience we can have of it. Degrees of contact range from being misted by warm steam sprays in San Antonio's HemisFair Park, or being splashed by the waterfall walkway in downtown Seattle, to being completely immersed in the Sebatu bathing pits or the caldaria of Bath. Immersion is a kind of escape, a form of disconnection from the world above the surface. John Cheever wrote about a troubled man who tried to escape the disappointments of life by swimming across his stuffy New England suburb, swimming pool by swimming pool. Contact with water can signal entrance into religious composure: Muslims wash their feet and hands before entering a mosque, and some Christians dab 'holy' water on their forehead upon entering a church. There is also something about contact with water that frees our inhibitions and spirits, just as it did for Gene Kelly in *Singin' in the Rain* or Fellini's cinematic Venus in the Trevi Fountain in *La Dolce Vita*.

Water meant for contact should, through its architecture, send out messages of invitation. It is essential that a fountain's pipes, lights and wires be safely concealed. Nothing is worse than to see the mechanical innards of a fountain or pool, especially when the water is turned off in cold seasons or dry spells. Water should seem alive, so that people do not feel as if they are standing in a limp shower or swimming in a stagnant pool. The pools at Sebatu are always kept in motion so that they charge the water with vitality and freshness. The upsurging jets of the Fountain Place, Dallas, are beacons for people to approach, challenge the water and sacrifice their dryness.

To invite contact, still water must seem fresh, clear, sparkling and clean, full of messages of beauty and health. An effective way to achieve this is to fill the water with dancing colour. Ricardo Legorreta uses solid planes of vibrant colour to make the water seem especially pure, a trick used by Arquitectonica and Victor

Carrasco with similar success. Pools, like those in Maui, shimmer in the sun by day and are dramatically illuminated at night so that the colours, patterns and reflections pulsate as if alive, inviting people to descend.

In *Rome and a Villa*, Eleanor Clark writes about the Trevi Fountain:

This is the last, royal chamber of the dream; the immersion is complete, more obviously so from the basin's being below street level like the boat in Piazza di Spagna; the stepping down is part of the imaginative process, like the descent into wells and pools in fairy tales, after which you feel no serious distinction of kind between the ocean characters of the fountains and the promenade hour swarms . . . The piazza is engulfed.

If the Barcaccia and the Trevi were lifted above people's downward gazes and onto a podium, they would lose their qualities of separation from normal life in the streets. Descent heightens our removal from the world at large. A considerable part of the magic in Paris and San Antonio is that people can move below the street level of the city to the plane of the river, heightening the feeling of escape and disconnection. Similarly, visitors to the Tokyo Sea Life Park descend from the surface above to the underwater spectacle, and the grotto at Stourhead brings us closer to the mystery of the water source.

While contact with water is an essential and popular aspect of many designs, in some places physical contact has little to do with its spirit. These days, vigilant guards turn away fountain jumpers who come to the Trevi expecting a swim. Few people would consider the idea of swimming in Monet's pond or the pools at the humble Administrator's Garden. Their still waters, not quite stagnant, but certainly murky, do not convey a sense of being fit for swimming. Splashing around the pensive reflecting pools at the Lincoln Memorial, the Taj Mahal or the Brion Cemetery would disrupt their serene dignity and blaspheme their sacred intentions, just as skinny-dipping at Stourhead would disturb its tranquillity.

Emotional contact with water occurs when people are allowed to get as close as possible without actually touching it, resulting in our famous 'mental leaning out over.' The most important thing to consider when making designs involving emotional contact with water is the edge. San Antonio is one of the most exemplary cases of communicative contact with a river. Even though the river is sunken in a winding corridor, people can walk along its sidewalks and cross on its low bridges. Often the river is only a few steps away with only a curb marking the distinction between land and water. The Fort Worth Water Gardens would not

Moore Ruble Yudell, Kobe Nishiokamoto, Kobe, Japan

be as delightful if people were prevented from getting close to the water. Handrails and barriers would make it seem too safe. Visitors may choose to safely watch from above as the water rushes into the pit, or from below as it rushes down at them.

From Paris to Tokyo to Fort Worth, every drop of water on the planet takes part in the water cycle. This guarantees that all water is connected in a continuous global chain, so that water never remains an isolated incident and never exclusively belongs to any specific time or place. Even the tiniest drop of water shares a heritage with the greatest ocean. If we could trace water's movement, we might see water pooling in Kyoto reappear in Hong Kong harbour, or water gushing from the Trevi Fountain resurface at the Villa d'Este.

The spirit of the Trevi is a celebration of the entire water cycle, personified by Oceanus, who commands the release, distribution, collection and evaporation of the Earth's water. In the words of its architect Nicola Salvi, the fountain 'shows the essential mobility of water, which never ceases in its operation and is incapable of ever remaining still, even for the briefest moment.' In Kyoto, the image of the bamboo fountain represents the arrival of water from the vast bodies of water circulating beyond the small garden. 'Eternity consists of opposites,' Seneca wrote, and to understand the oceanic infinities is to appreciate the finite flume. This is equally true for Kahn's Salk Institute plaza, where the thin vein evokes the inevitable return of water to the oceanic receptacle. The Neptune pool at San Simeon is stirring because we see that, although it is enormous, when compared to the ocean it represents only a minute drop. The Ryoan-ji stone garden performs the greatest feat by making us think of water when we only see stones. Contained in the rectangular plot is a profoundly simple view of the ocean, perfectly balanced, perfectly harmonious.

Finally, we return to Sen no Rikyu's legendary tea garden. Inside its hedge, visitors would have heard the subliminal murmurs of an unseen sea. In the stone font, people would have dipped their hands in the water, perhaps seeing their own reflection rippling across the tiny mirror. Comparing the few cups of water with the limited view of the sea invested the garden with a subtle but resounding message: that every drop of water in the world is connected with all the rest. It was a masterful combination of the senses. Through the careful arrangement of water and architecture, we can create for ourselves a place in the nature surrounding us – a place like Fallingwater, the Hearst pool, the Salk Institute, the Kyoto basins, or the Trevi – connected to the cycle, and all of the world's water.

Reprinted from *Architecture and Water* by Charles Moore and Jane Lidz. Published in 1994 by Harry N Abrams Inc, New York. All Rights Reserved.

Moore Ruble Yudell, Kobe
Nishiokamoto, Kobe, Japan

COOP HIMMELB(L)AU

VIDEO CLIP FOLLY
Groningen, The Netherlands

The Video Clip Folly, a presentation space for 40 persons, stresses both the diversity of contemporary architecture and that video is of special interest to the city's museum. Initiated by the city planning commission and the Groningen Museum of Art it was completed in 1990 and now stands in the Dampster Diep canal, alongside projects by Peter Eisenman, Zaha Hadid, Rem Koolhaas and Bernard Tschumi. Despite its temporary appearance, it is a permanent structure celebrating the 950th anniversary of Groningen, and will be incorporated into the planned extension to the existing museum.

The box, as a form, has been fought against, often destroyed and yet returns again and again as a stubborn element in Coop Himmelb(l)au ideas. Here it carries the obvious seams of construction, like jewellery. These traces of production are transformed into tattoos, symbolic signs, a type of technological primitivism. The box's rough surface is appropriate, as the structural framework is constructed from industrial elements, their coarse finishes retained, and their uninhibited anarchism is sculptural in nature. It is a harsh structure that invites one to see the conflicts within its construction, the movement between its elements.

The construction consists of a movable box, supports and a walkway that terminates in a viewing platform under a roof of pierced waves, which demonstrates the simplest way of creating a space in our culture. The viewing platform is open on all sides apart from the one which is a solid plane, tilted towards the platform, that acts as a visual block. Instead the view is replaced with four video screens. Around these components is the box that is able to travel, on a rail parallel to the walkway, towards, or away, from the end wall. The effect of this movement is quite dramatic as it alters the platform's exposure, changing it from an internal to an external space. This action creates a dark cave for the video pictures, and then releases the viewer from its embrace. It has a unique ability to articulate and define the boundaries of the space in response to requirements. For instance, it surrounds the visitor completely during rock video, but remains open during erotic videos. It is a building capable of interchanging the conventional delineation of public and private spheres.

The video folly is architecture rather than a high-tech answer to a technological medium. It is an exhibition pavilion, showing a synthesis of film and music, whose strategies it imitates. For instance, it reflects the emotional qualities of video by standing on its own two legs, demonstrates space by moving a simple box, creates darkness in order to see and interchanges private and public.

The Video Clip Folly advertises a culture it is part of and in the manner of video clips it is an institution, not a product. It entices one away from isolation, using its 'spectacular' qualities, into public life, and makes one aware of an aspect of reality that is usually swallowed up by uninterrupted television, and living room noises.

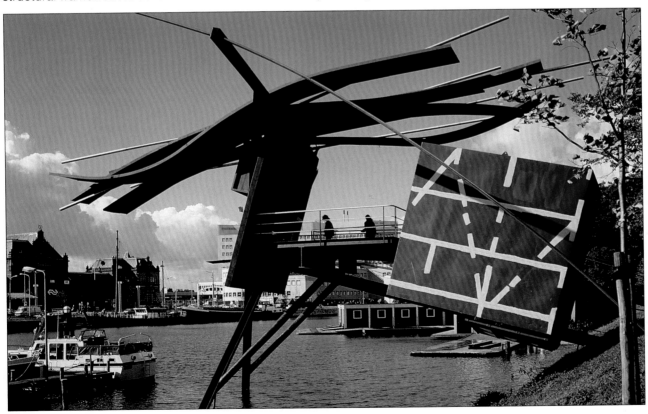

GRONINGER MUSEUM OF ART
Groningen, The Netherlands

Coop Himmelb(l)au was also commissioned to design part of the new Groninger Museum of Art, of which the Video Folly will be part. This extension was started in summer 1993 and was opened at the end of October last year. The building will be 10,000 square feet and house works from the 16th century until the present day.

The concept is based on the idea of the unfolding of positive and negative space, the continuation of the rooftop structure over the river bank and across the water. The internal gallery spaces, part of the larger museum complex, are designed by Alessandro Mendini, Milan.

The broken shell
The cut mass evokes a lot of broken volumes.
Along the sectional lines it shows the different layers of skin.
The broken skin allows the inside to come out, as well as the outside to fold inwards.

The liquid innerspace
Similar to the soft consistency of the brain, towards the inside light but towards the outside well covered by its skull, the organisation of the interior presents complex circulation systems asking for different points of view and provoking different figures of movement.

Different levels to conceive art
The 'inside-skin', working as a flexible exhibition surface, as well as the circulation that leads onto varying levels, allows different points of view for looking at the artwork.

Structural model
Cutting through the potential volume certain design principles can be read:
– the tangent circulation-systems
– the partial centralization of space
The functional sketch becomes a penetrating figure within the spatial concept.

The built negative space
The dissolving volume
Either volumes placed in a light-space or volumes of light cutting through mass.

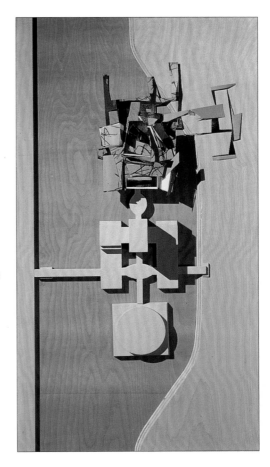

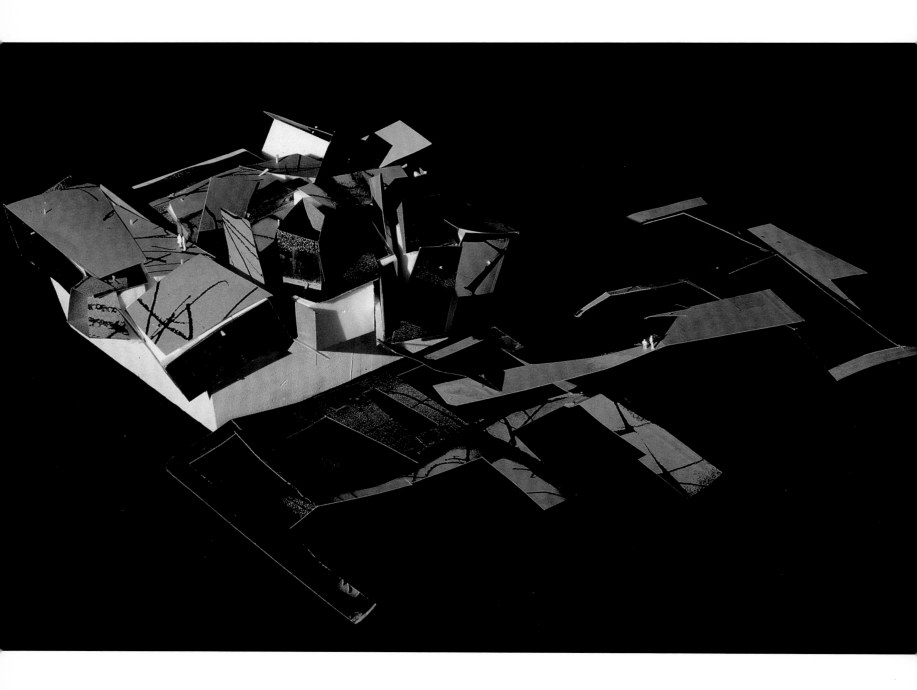

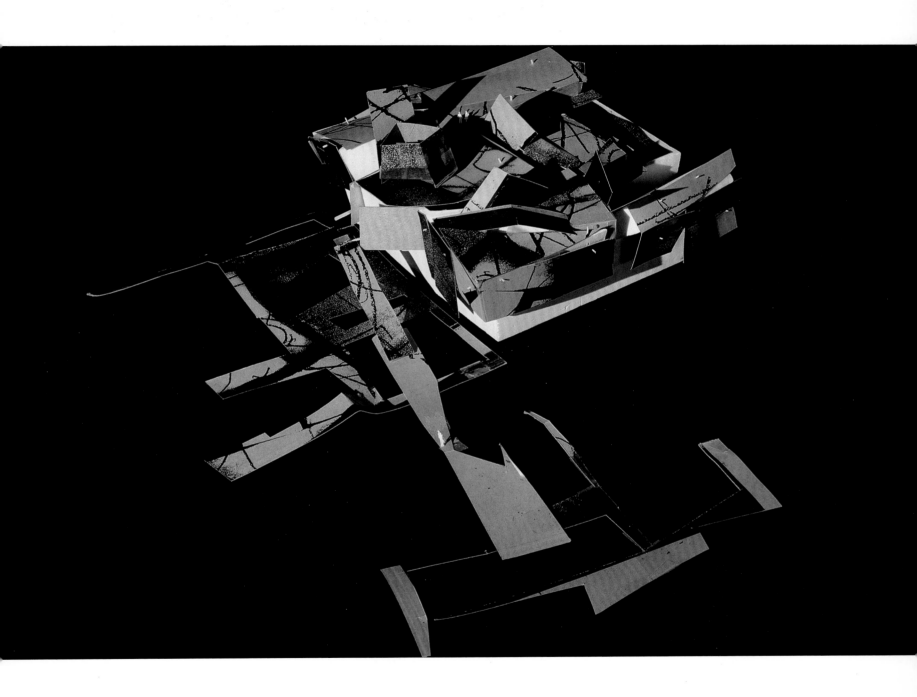

NICHOLAS GRIMSHAW
BRITISH PAVILION, EXPO 92
Seville

Nicholas Grimshaw & Partners won the competition to design a pavilion to reflect the spirit of Britain at Expo 92, in Seville. The limited competition arose from, the then prime minister, Baroness Thatcher's stated aim that the UK pavilion was to be 'quite the best', and would demonstrate the qualities of Britain to Europe and the rest of the world.

The intention behind the initial competition entry was to create a place of coolness and rest on the Expo site, in contrast with the more Disney-like aspects of the event. Climate, method of construction and programme were to determine the kit of parts approach; a primary aim being that the design of the building would moderate temperature extremes before any mechanical cooling was used.

The building itself was to serve as an advertisement for British industry, and so the structure was constructed with components made in Britain, and transported to the site. This determined the use of manufactured, lightweight materials, the opposite of the heavy masonry commonly used in hot countries to control heat. The, white painted, tubular steel structure is designed to have no site welding, and so structural elements are pin jointed. Apart from the concrete foundations, the building was almost entirely prefabricated in Britain.

The structure encloses a large, single volume and supports different types of external 'skin' that respond to conditions of the climate, according to their orientation to the sun. The eastern elevation is the focal point of the building, animated by a water wall, 65 metres long and 18 metres high, which is powered by solar panels on the roof. The building's structure is internal, and on the outside water adheres to the glass, forming rhythmic patterns as it runs down the surface. The environmental purpose is to create an intermediate zone of coolness. The water cools the immediate environment by reducing the surface temperature of the glass, thus reducing radiant heat into the building; whilst, the water spray cools the surrounding air by evaporative cooling.

On the western wall, which receives sun during the hottest part of the day, stacks of shipping containers, filled with water, provide the thermal capacity traditionally achieved with masonry. The north and south walls use another technology, imported from outside traditional building construction. PVC coated polyester fabric, made in the manner of yacht sails, is fixed to bowed-steel tubes as sails are to masts, using luff grooves. A second layer of sailcloth in angled louvre-like strips provides additional protection from the sun, on the south elevation. All of these techniques are passive, except the solar powered pumps, and require no external input of energy to function. Their combined effect is to reduce the internal temperature by 10°C which, in Seville, can mean the difference between unbearable and pleasant conditions. Localised air conditioning provides additional comfort in the self-contained pods accommodating the audiovisual displays, as required by the brief. The public entered the building through the water wall, over a small entrance bridge, and were then guided through the exhibition spaces on a series of travel-ators and walkways.

Water has been used throughout this scheme in two particular ways. It is both a visual device that enhances the building's aesthetic appeal, and also used as a highly successful, and innovative, method of climatic control.

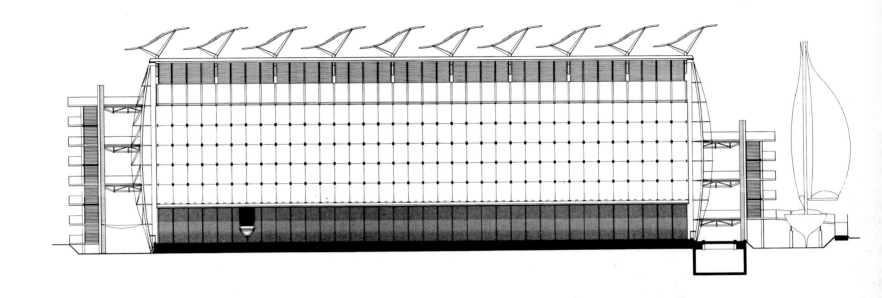

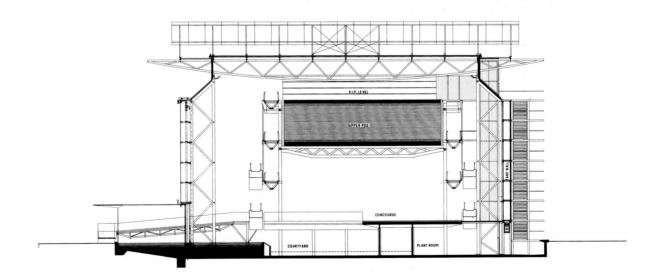

Section and elevation

STEVEN HOLL
STRETTO HOUSE
Texas

Sited adjacent to three spring-fed ponds, with existing concrete dams, the house reflects the character of the site in a series of concrete blocks, or 'spatial dams', with a metal framed, or 'aqueous space', flowing through them. Flowing over the dams, like the overlapping stretto in music, the water is a reflection of the landscape outside as well as the virtual overlapping of the spaces inside.

Bartok's *Music for Strings, Percussion and Celeste* provides the stretto on which the house form was based. Consisting of four movements, the piece has a distinct division between heavy, percussion, and light, strings. Where music has a solidity in instrumentation and sound the house attempts an analogue in light and space. The building is formed in four sections, each consisting of two modes; heavy orthogonal masonry and light and curvi-linear metal. The concrete block and metal recall Texas vernacular. The plan is orthogonal whilst the section is curvilin-ear. However, the guest house inverts this; the plan is curvilinear and section orthogonal. This reflects similar inver-sions in the first movement of the Bartok score. In the main house 'aqueous space' is developed by several means; floor planes pull the level of one space into the next, roof planes pull space over walls and an arched wall pulls light down from a skylight. Materials and details continue the spatial concepts in poured concrete, glass cast in fluid shapes, slumped glass and liquid terrazzo.

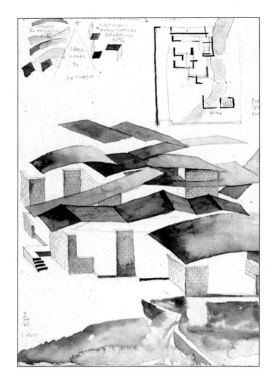

*LEFT TO RIGHT: Exploratory
sketch; watercolour of flooded room
(space and detail study)*

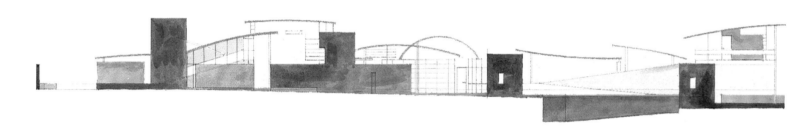

*ABOVE: Concept sketch; BELOW:
Overview of model*

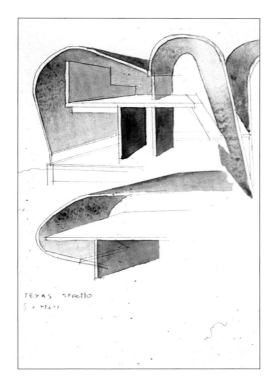

LEFT TO RIGHT: Exploratory sketch; watercolour of interior (space and detail study)

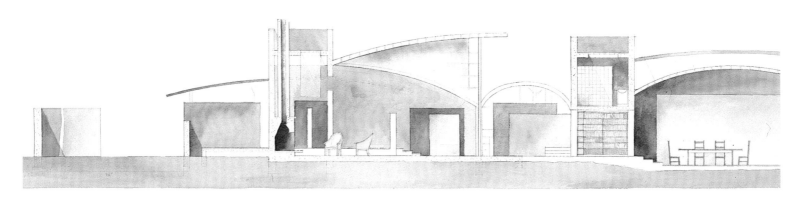

ABOVE: Watercolour of exterior elevation (space and detail study)

CHIASMA - HELSINKI MUSEUM OF CONTEMPORARY ART
Helsinki, Finland

The site for the new museum lies in the heart of Helsinki, at the foot of the Parliament building to the west, with Eliel Saarinen's Helsinki Station to the east and Alvar Aalto's Finlandia Hall to the north. The challenging character of this site stems from the confluence of the various city grids and from the triangular shape that opens to Töölö Bay in the distance.

The concept of Chiasma involves the intertwining of the building's mass with the geometry of the city and landscape. An implicit cultural line curves to link the building to the Finlandia Hall while it engages a 'natural line' that connects it to the landscape and Töölö Bay. The bay has been extended up to the building and will provide an area for future civic development along this tapering body of water, while also serving as a reflecting pool for the Finlandia Hall and new development along the South edge of the water. The horizontal light, of the northern latitudes, is enhanced by a waterscape that will serve as an urban mirror linking the new museum to Helsinki's Töölö heart. The changes in elevation proposed with the water extension, and its shallow depth, would allow for parking decks and highway linkages which are presently part of various planning considerations.

This water extension from the Bay intertwines with and passes through the new museum. The rectangular water which is proposed along the west elevation of the new building is the source of a slow recirculating system which lowers the water level gradually from three metres elevation to the base level of the bay. The gentle sound of moving water can be heard when walking through the cusp of the building section which will remain open for passage all year round. These ponds are not intended to be drained as is conventional in Finland. Instead, they will be allowed to freeze in winter, utilising a detail devised by Eliel Saarinen that allows the water's inevitable expansion during freezing. At night the west pond would reflect the internal light radiating from the museum which has been designed to express a 'spatiality of night'. During the early evening hours of the winter months, glowing light escaping from the interior of the building along the west facade would invite the public in.

The design for the Helsinki Museum of Contemporary Art attempts to provide a variety of spatial experiences to accommodate the variety of styles that artists are now exploring. The general character of the rooms, almost rectangular with one wall curved, allows for a silent yet dramatic backdrop for the exhibition of contemporary art. These rooms are meant to be silent, but not static.

The slight variation in room size and shape allows the horizontal, natural light to enter in several different ways and drives movement through a series of spatial sequences. In this regard the overall design becomes a slightly warped 'gallery of rooms', where the spatial flow emerges from the combination of the horizontal light-catching section and the fluidity of the internal space. This curving, unfolding sequence provides elements of both mystery and surprise, which does not exist in traditional arrangements. Instead, the visitor is confronted with a continuous unfolding of an infinite series of changing perspectives which connect the internal experience to the overall concept of intertwining, or Chiasma.

This open-ended spatial system suggests an expanse that lies beyond, unlike orthogonal and 'centred' compositions. The spaces of the intertwining curves avoid both the rigidity of a classical approach and the excessive complexity of expressionism. The dynamic internal circulation, with its curving ramps and stairs, allows for an open interactive viewing, empowering the visitor to choose their own route through the galleries. Rather than hierarchical sequencing or ordering, this open-ended casual circulation provokes moments of pause, reflection and discovery.

With this scheme there is the potential to confirm that architecture, art and culture are not separate disciplines, but are an integral part of the city and the landscape. Through care in the development of details and materials, the new museum will provide a dynamic yet subtle spatial form, extending towards the city in the south and the landscape to the north. The geometry has an interior mystery, and an exterior horizon which, like two hands clasping each other, form the architectonic equivalent of a public invitation. In referring back to the landscape, the interiors are reversible, forming the site which in this special place, and circumstance, is a synthesis of building and landscape . . . a Chiasma.

OPPOSITE, FROM ABOVE LEFT TO RIGHT: Watercolour of interior; watercolour of interior looking towards Finlandia Hall; views of model; detail of model; computer montage of building on site

45

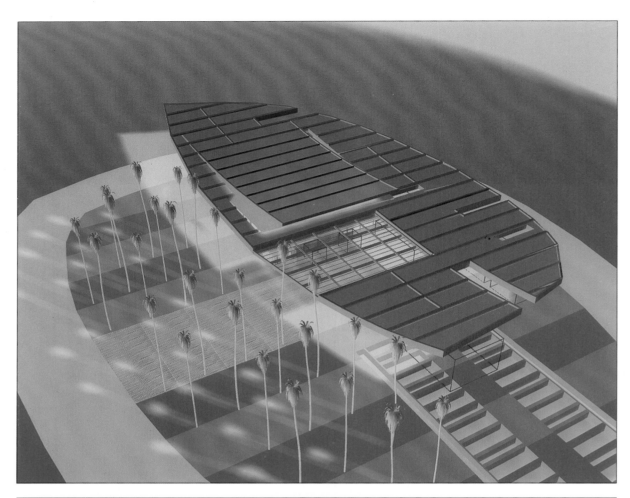

MEHRDAD YAZDANI
FILTRATION PLANT
Los Angeles

Whilst design principal at Ellerbe Becket Mehrdad Yazdani designed a filtration plant, for the Department of Water and Power. The scheme was to propose not only a specific building, but also a potentially prototypical architectural design for future developments. The new design amends an earlier version by the in-house engineers. The scheme aims to organise the plant's building components and exterior spatial relationships while maintaining a sympathetic rapport with the surrounding environment.

Set in a canyon north of Beverly Hills, surrounded by affluent residential communities, the building presents a direct response to the sensitive challenge of placing an entirely new industrial facility in a natural non-industrial setting. Seen from hillside homes the primary impact is the clear visibility of the plant's varied structures and roofs. The design creates landscaped roofs, 'disguising' the building components beneath, that maintain a harmonious coexistence with natural surroundings. The structure's shapes conform to, and echo architecturally the topography of neighbouring hills. Within the building the various roof cuts allow light and air to penetrate the spaces below and provide access to the roof.

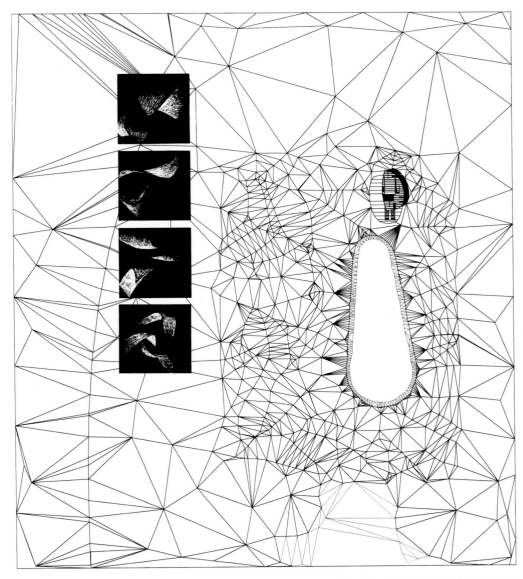

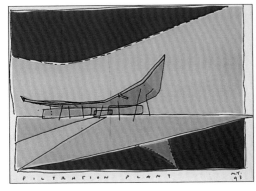

OPPOSITE: Computer generated images of building; FROM ABOVE LEFT TO RIGHT: Site plan; concept painting, Mehrdad Yazdani; view of conceptual model

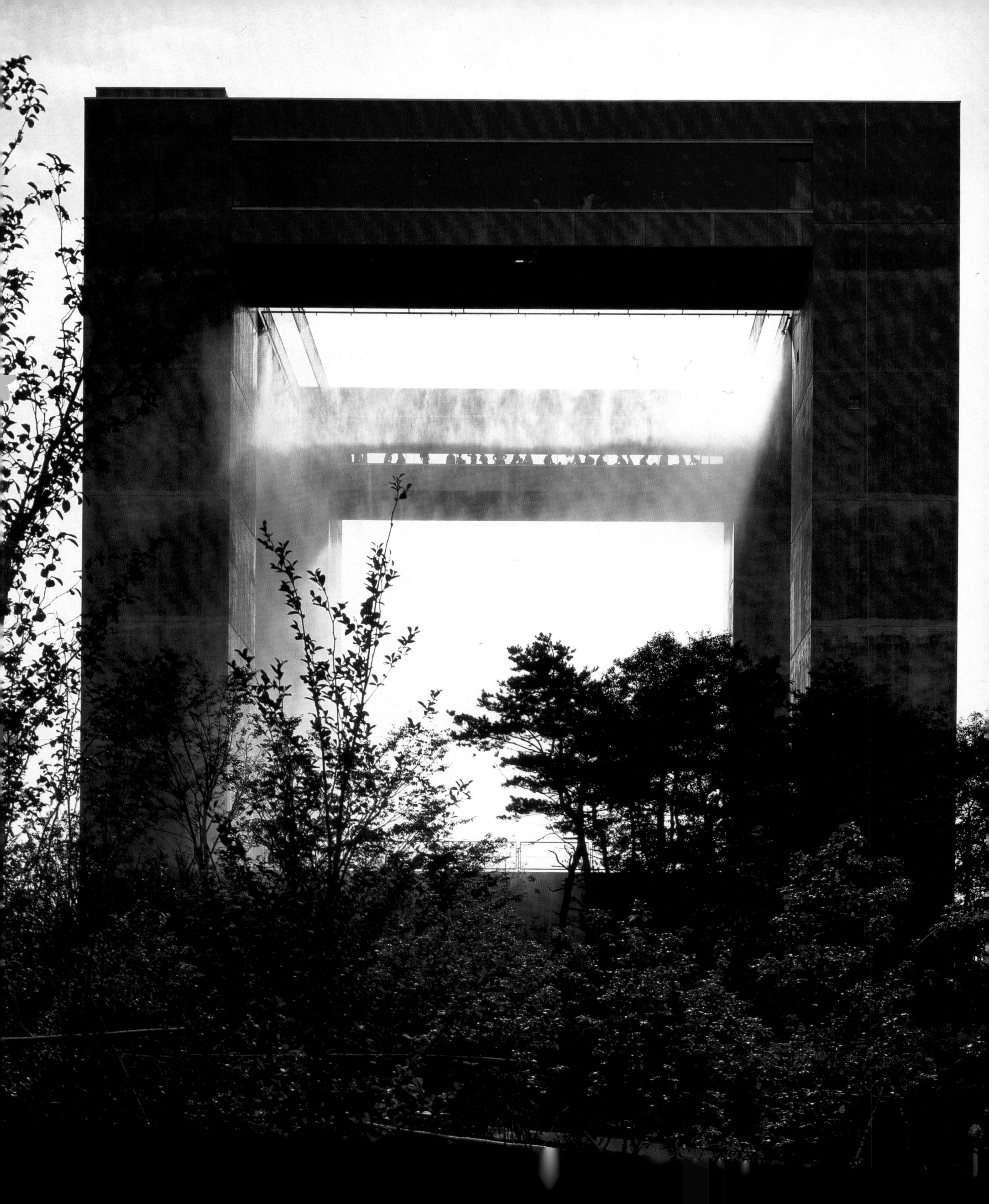

SHOEI YOH
PROSPECTA 92
Toyama, Japan

Prospecta '92 is a memorial building for the first Japanese Expo, held in Toyama in 1992. Temporarily this structure served as one of the Exposition pavilions, however now it serves as an example of how architecture can be endowed with life. It allows the visitors to become at one with nature. The theme for the exposition was the metamorphosis of 'water', as Toyama is well known for its crisp water from the snowy mountains.

The building is an observatory which is designed for the pure appreciation of natural phenomena and the beautiful landscape. It stands on four large concrete columns: two enclosing elevators, two encasing stairways. The viewer is able to see snowy mountains as well as various natural phenomena like rainbows, fog, clouds, lightning and shooting stars, in a cubic frame which helps natural perception. Instinctive perception and intelligent understanding of nature through natural perception has been Yoh's lifelong theme.

Water is life and the circulation of water is mysterious: rain, waterfall, cascade, river, the sea, evaporation, clouds and snow, the way rain reflects sunlight forming rainbows, and how people perceive that the irregular forms of fog are dancing in accordance with the music that is performed; some people even see the illusion of a dragon dancing.

The movement of natural phenomena is supposed to affect our instinct rather than intelligence. The more intelligent we are, the less instinctive we tend to be. Whilst recovering such senses we feel that time is very short, as we are supposed to be syncopating movement as a part of natural phenomena.

Explanatory section; OVERLEAF FROM L TO R: Computer generated axonometric; section; first floor plan; second floor plan

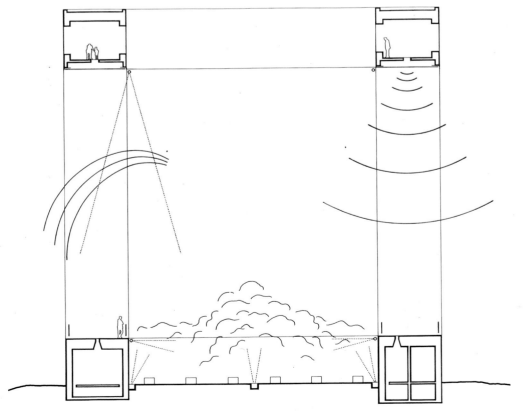

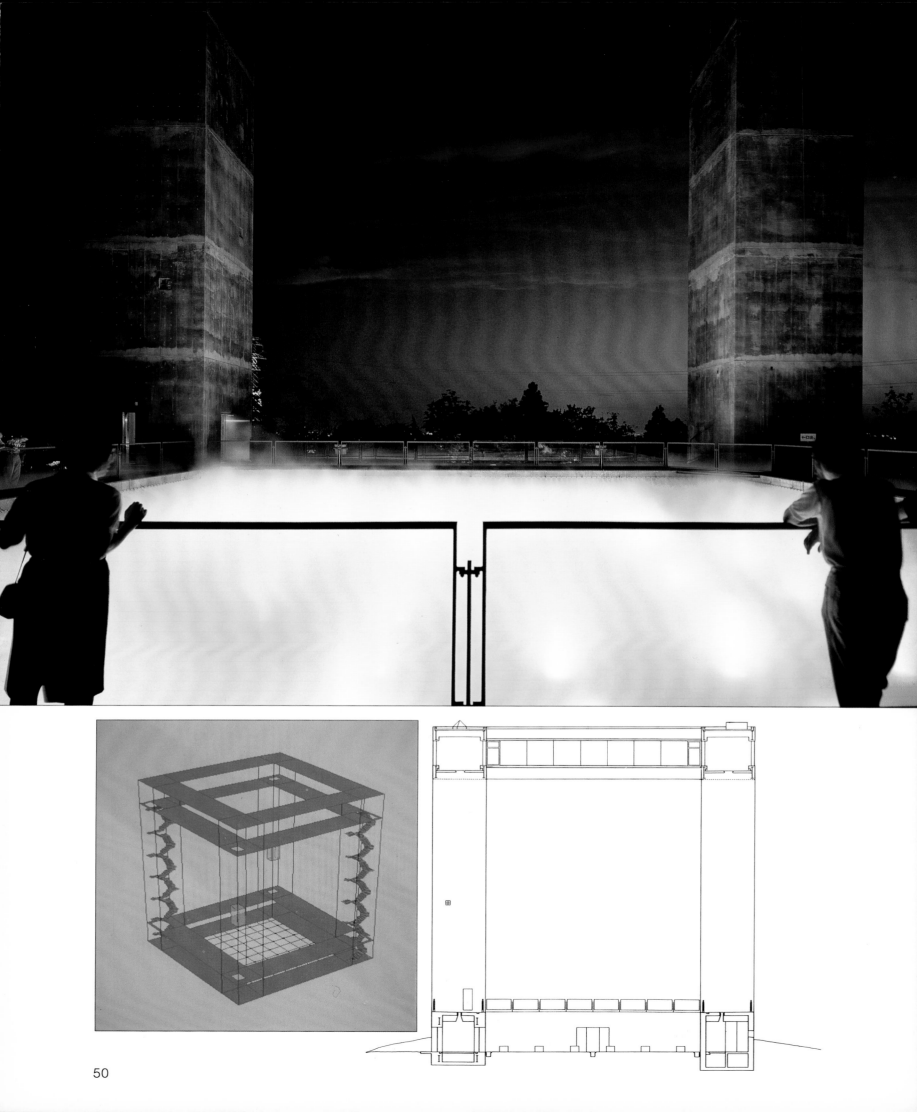

51

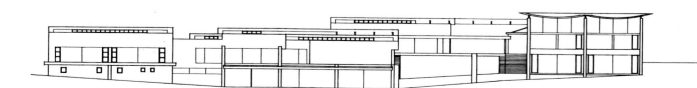

ARASHIYAMA GOLF CLUB
Okinawa Island

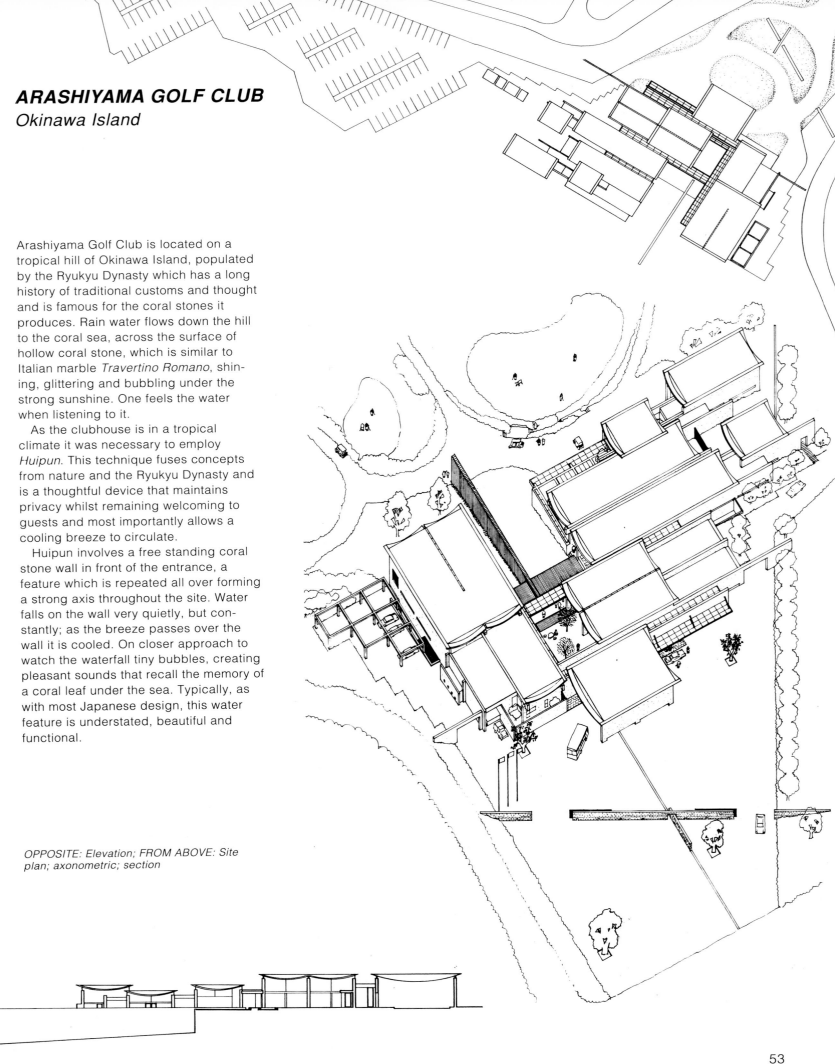

Arashiyama Golf Club is located on a tropical hill of Okinawa Island, populated by the Ryukyu Dynasty which has a long history of traditional customs and thought and is famous for the coral stones it produces. Rain water flows down the hill to the coral sea, across the surface of hollow coral stone, which is similar to Italian marble *Travertino Romano*, shining, glittering and bubbling under the strong sunshine. One feels the water when listening to it.

As the clubhouse is in a tropical climate it was necessary to employ *Huipun*. This technique fuses concepts from nature and the Ryukyu Dynasty and is a thoughtful device that maintains privacy whilst remaining welcoming to guests and most importantly allows a cooling breeze to circulate.

Huipun involves a free standing coral stone wall in front of the entrance, a feature which is repeated all over forming a strong axis throughout the site. Water falls on the wall very quietly, but constantly; as the breeze passes over the wall it is cooled. On closer approach to watch the waterfall tiny bubbles, creating pleasant sounds that recall the memory of a coral leaf under the sea. Typically, as with most Japanese design, this water feature is understated, beautiful and functional.

OPPOSITE: Elevation; FROM ABOVE: Site plan; axonometric; section

ARTHUR ERICKSON

JOHOR COASTAL DEVELOPMENT
Johor Bahru, Malaysia

In 1993 construction on the Johor Coastal Development was instigated. The site is situated at the southern tip of Malaysia and comprises three-and-a-half kilometres of prime shoreline, of which 120 acres is of marine reclamation. The scheme is a large-scale development with major public amenities and includes 1,560 mid- and up-market condominium units in an attractive marine park setting.

The master plan inorporates a strip of new land, adjacent to the Coast Road, and a number of separate, offshore, residential islands, conceived as a contemporary reinterpretation of traditional Malaysian water villages. Vehicular circulation is limited to the inland edge of the site, while a landscaped public promenade runs along the water edge.

The inland development area is projected as a verdant landscape of hills and valleys, with luxuriant planting on every floor and intensive ground level landscaping that integrates the various freestanding buildings. Much of the inland residential development is accommodated in eight to ten storey, back-to-back, terraced structures, each with its own internal, naturally ventilated atrium space. The linear atrium buildings are framed by four 16-storey towers, each with an open core, hanging gardens and other features to moderate the climate and induce natural ventilation.

The six-and seven-storey offshore islands are also terraced in form, with a landscaped recreation area on the roof, and private boat moorage directly beneath the units. All residential units are treated as 'villas in the sky' with their own private 'hanging gardens'. The identity of the units is enhanced by a cellular architectural expression.

Views of model accommodation islands

EPPICH HOUSE
Vancouver, Canada

Completed in 1988, and located on a south facing slope, the residence was designed for the owner of a manufacturing firm, specializing in metal fabrication. The intent was to construct a steel and glass building using the materials, and labour available at the plant.

The 7,000 square-foot structure comprises three levels, set at right angles to the slope of the site. The main living level, including pool and recreation facilities, separates the children's level, below, from the parents' level, above. This higher level overlooks the enclosed swimming pool structure, which is perpendicular to the main building mass.

The other two levels are perched on terraces, cut parallel to the site, and retained by stone planter walls. Each level terminates in a half vault greenhouse space, constructed of glass blocks for privacy from neighbouring residences. Glass and aluminium wall panels are broken by stainless steel columns, which support the white steel structural beams. The hard external materials contrast with the softer interior finishes.

To complete the composition – the series of pools – on each of the terraces above, a creek, bordering the south end of the site was diverted to create a reflecting pool.

CALIFORNIA PLAZA
Los Angeles

California Plaza was a winning entry in an international architect and developer competition for the redevelopment of 11 acres of land, approximately four downtown city blocks, in the Bunker Hill redevelopment area, Los Angeles. The proposal includes over 300,000 square metres of office space, 750 units of condominium housing, a 400-room luxury hotel, 25,000 square metres of retail space and a 10,000 square-metre Museum of Contemporary Arts.

The scheme's urban design concept is to integrate its diverse uses into the surrounding area, and to provide an active link between the downtown office core and the Music Centre, at opposite ends of the site. The solution incorporates cultural, recreational and commercial activities which combine to create a new public and commercial focus for the greater Los Angeles region.

Construction began in 1983 and was completed in 1990, whilst the detailed design and construction of the Central Plaza, second office tower and Dance Gallery are now in progress. Completion of the entire development is anticipated within eight to ten years.

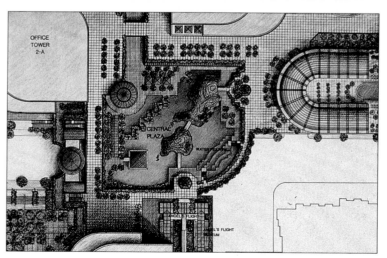

Site Plan

56

ROBSON SQUARE
Vancouver, Canada

Between 1978 and 1983, three blocks in downtown Vancouver were developed as an integrated complex of public uses, with major emphasis on open space and pedestrian amenities. At the north end of the project is the historic Courthouse, the symbolic centre of downtown Vancouver, which has now been converted by the city into the new home of the Vancouver Art Gallery. This neoclassical building was a major inspiration for the entire project and is used as a backdrop for the new buildings.

The middle block accommodates a city square, as well as the Provincial Government offices. It is designed as a low-rise terraced structure whose entire roof area is usable landscaped open space.

The pedestrian role of Robson Street, between the north and middle blocks, was strengthened by the elimination of all vehicular traffic, except surface transit, and the location of a number of public attractions. These include a tourist information centre, several small restaurants, skating rink, exhibition space, auditorium, meeting rooms and landscaped areas. This area of the project is the activity focus, both indoor and outdoor, of the city square, and a major magnet for the entire downtown core.

The new Law Courts on the south block now house the functions once crowded into the historic Courthouse. Like the new Government Office building, the new Law Courts have an open character that emphasises easy public access and avoids the formidable appearance of many similar buildings. Its design extends the north-south visual axis, and mid-block pedestrian route, which originate at the existing Courthouse. The building also maintain a relationship of scale with the old Courthouse, and forms a backdrop for the public open spaces developed in the middle of the complex.

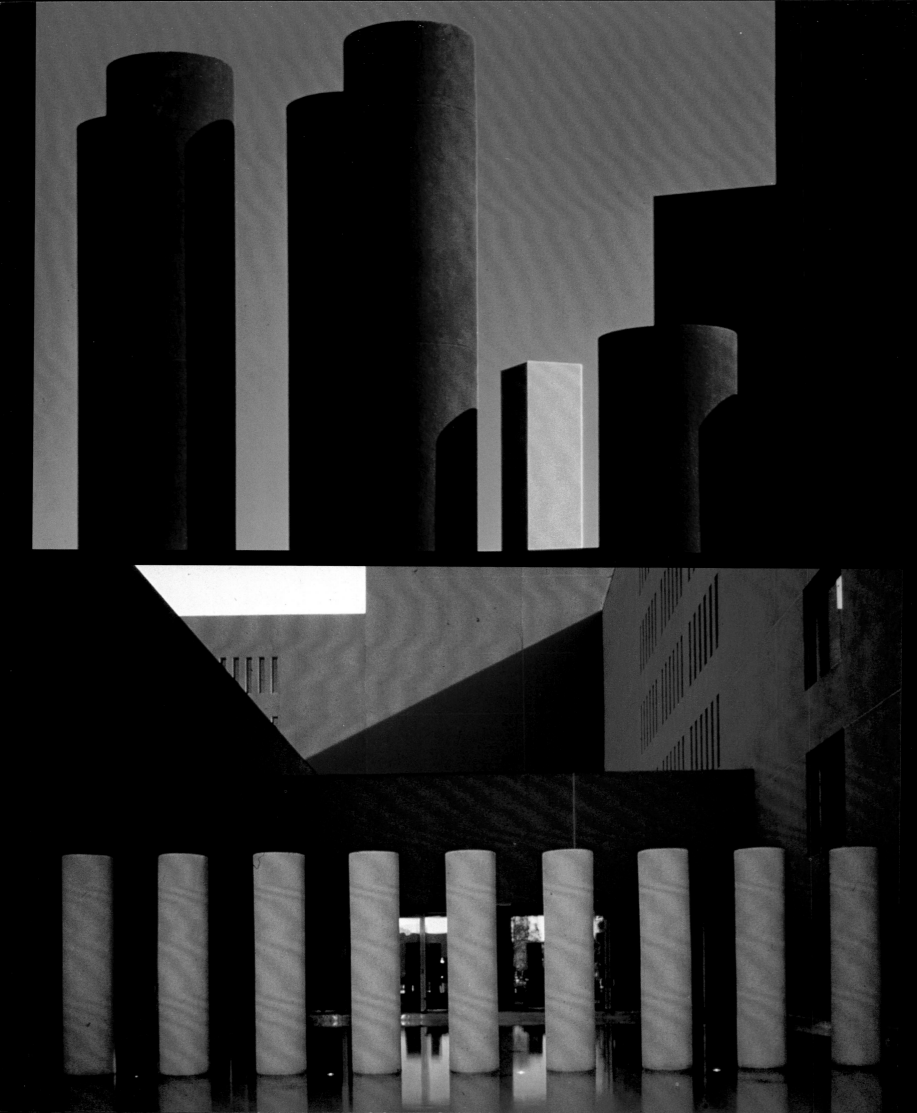

RICARDO LEGORRETA
SOLANA
Southlake, Texas

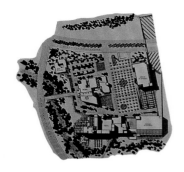

Dealing with a 1,900 acre property, of rolling hills, and the desire of the client, IBM, to design a unique scheme, a team of four architects, Mitchell Giurgola, Barton Mayers, Peter Walker and Legorreta Arquitectos, developed a very simple scheme that took advantage of the highway and underpass that crossed the property. The design concept is a series of buildings and courtyards incorporating and recovering, the surrounding prairie, the highway and underpass to create individual and intimate spaces.

Completed in 1991, the compounds established their unity by the interplay of the scale of limiting walls, height, colour and the proportions of the fenestration. This concept permits an overall continuity for the project, whilst retaining each architect's artistic freedom. Vertical elements were created as directional and entrance symbols, and careful use of walls, textures and colours humanised the limitless scale of the Texas land-scape.

The village centre consists of two office buildings, a shopping and office com-pound, a hotel and a health and sports club. The IBM building consists of 34,838 square metres of offices, dining rooms and a computer centre.

Site plan

CAMINO REAL HOTEL
Ixtapa, Mexico

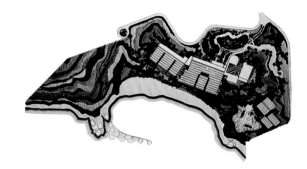

Finished in 1981, the Camino Real Hotel's site selection was done from the sea looking towards the shore. At the time Ricardo Legorreta stated 'this is a marvellous spot and it requires an exceptional hotel.' The land possesses a strong personality from which the entire project evolves. The imposing sea, combined with an extraordinary coastline and rugged mountain range, was essential to the hotel. The hotel adapts to the site's topography and vegetation obtaining the maximum benefit from its environment. Once this design constraint had been established the hotel developed naturally in terraces that adapted to the mountainous slopes.

Three different environments were created in the hotel: the enclosed sleeping quarters; a covered terrace suitable for dining, resting or socialising that weaves easily from the sleeping area, and is separated by ingenious sliding louvred doors and lastly an open patio that extends outward to the Mexican Pacific. To create as natural an environment as possible these areas, on the whole, rely on natural ventilation. Also rather than a typical swimming pool area, the design offers an assortment of walls, aqueducts, roofs and fountains that surround both sunbathers and swimmers. The beach, however, was left untouched, the only structures being palapas, palm thatched umbrellas, that blend with the surf and sand.

The hotel site recalls the forgotten pleasures of walking. The environs of the Camino Real, overlooking a picturesque cove, are laced with paths and stairways for those who wish to stroll through this magical setting. For those less inclined there are elevators to the beach. Lastly, it should be mentioned that Camino Real is truly Mexican and reflects the culture's spirit, forms, colours, building materials and furnishings. In short, like a visualised contemporary Mexico, it is strong, spacious, romantic and spiritually powerful.

Site plan

REGINA HOTEL
Cancun, Mexico

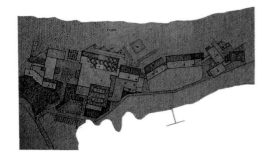

The climate, the water and sand, the special form of the terrain and its position between the sea and the lagoon make Conrad Cancun a unique place and the Regina Hotel, completed in 1991, is well adapted to its location. It utilises simple and lengthened forms that permit the guests to enjoy, depending on the time of day, the spectacular views of either the sea or the lagoon. The design allows the guests to maintain a permanent relationship with the surrounding water. Like the Camino Real, the Regina takes advantage of the sea breezes and so the majority of the hotel is naturally ventilated, negating the need for air conditioning.

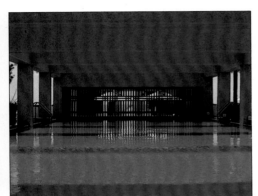

Site plan

61

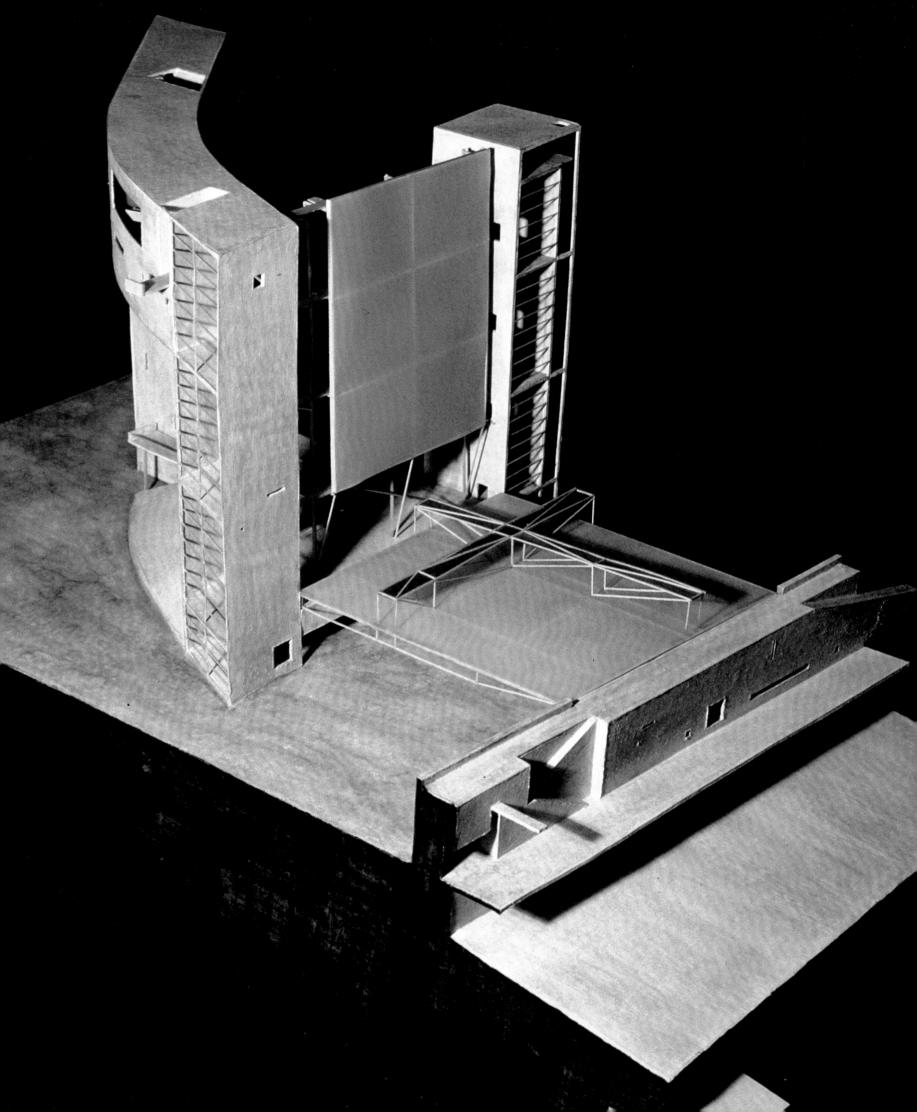

HANRAHAN & MEYERS
CANAL STREET WATERLINE
New York

A series of buildings is proposed along the west side of Manhattan with development concentrated in dense clusters at the significant cross-streets of the City; at 42nd Street, 34th Street, 14th Street and Canal Street. Designed in 1991, the detailed plan for the Canal Street Waterline shows three blocks which are proposed for future development. On the southern edge of the central block, the so-called 'hydroscraper', has been developed in significant detail.

The Canal Street Waterline is intended as a view of the future New York City exploring possibilities for urban space, new programmes for living and working and the relationship between the City and its environment. The scheme forges a connection between the inhabitants, technology, and the environment surrounding Manhattan; rivers and ocean.

A large open space is created in the centre of the Canal Street block, defined by the surrounding buildings and a screen for outdoor films. The screen links the interior of the City to an evolving waterfront park. As a spectacular visual element, this screen becomes the City's 'eye'. A School for the Performing Arts occupies the top floors of the curving wall building marking the western edge of the new Canal Street piazza. Performances by the students can be projected onto

this screen that separates the piazza from the waterfront.

Information for monitoring the City's environment is collected from the skin of the southern-most tower of this block. The tower collects information about the air, light and noise levels in the City. It houses the former Department of Docks and Piers which is now transformed into an environmental and social monitoring agency. The tower provides both a programmatic and physical link to the infrastructure intersecting the site, the Holland Tunnel and its ventilation shaft buildings to the west and the east. This relatively neutral tower of simple office space displays on its southern face an assembly of air, light and water monitoring equipment. As a building whose function is to monitor the environmental statistics of the City, the tower becomes the City's 'ear'. A figural element winds its way, like duct work, through the complex volumes of the City's 'ear', to appear as a singular disruption within the tower's west facade. This is a single-family residence for the City Statistician.

It was the architects' intention that open space, new technologies, and the idea of living in the air, suspended over water, define a new urban architecture for New York City which is embodied by the complexities of the development.

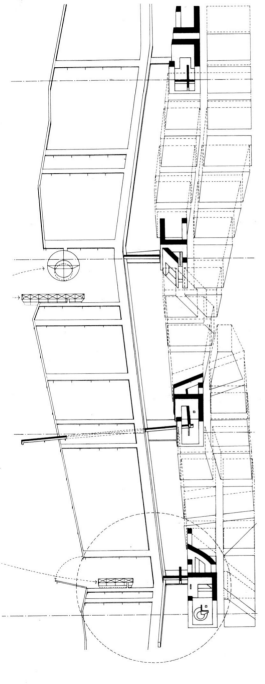

OPPOSITE: Aerial view of model; ABOVE: Diagram of future west side development

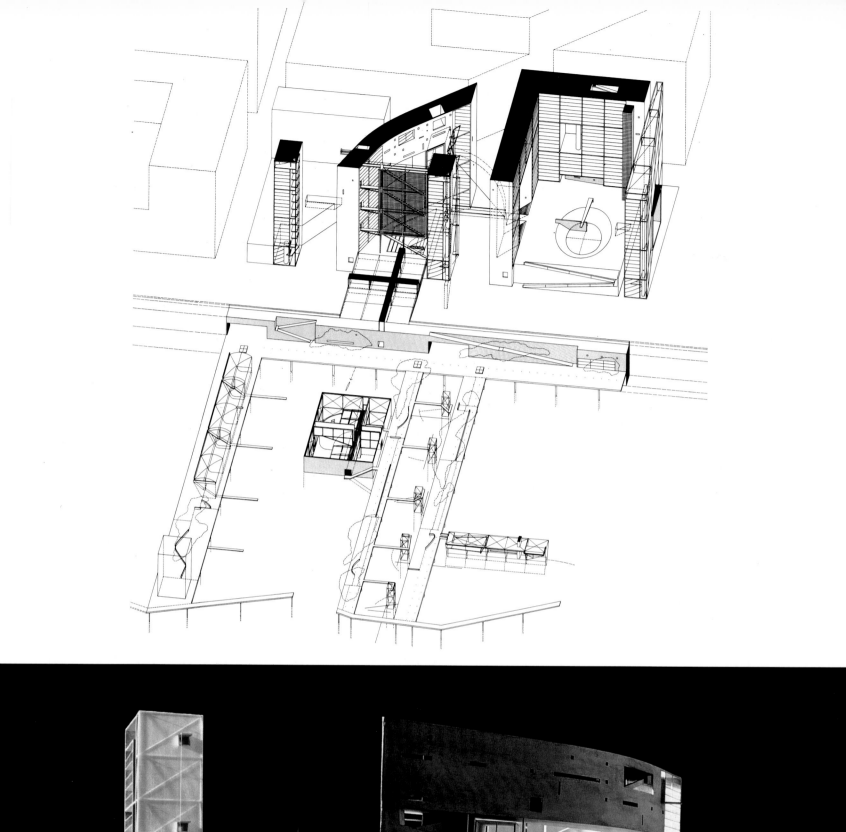

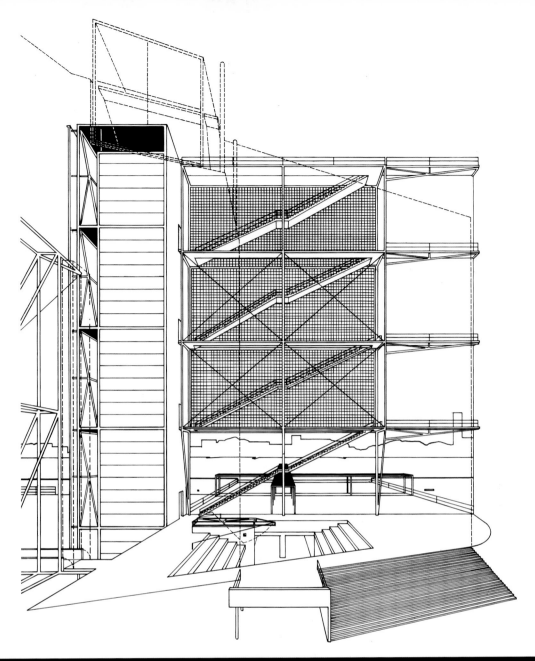

OPPOSITE, FROM ABOVE L TO R: Site axonometric looking east; model of 'Hydroscraper'; view from Canal Street into plaza; FROM ABOVE L TO R: Perspective; model of 'Hydroscraper'; view of model towards river

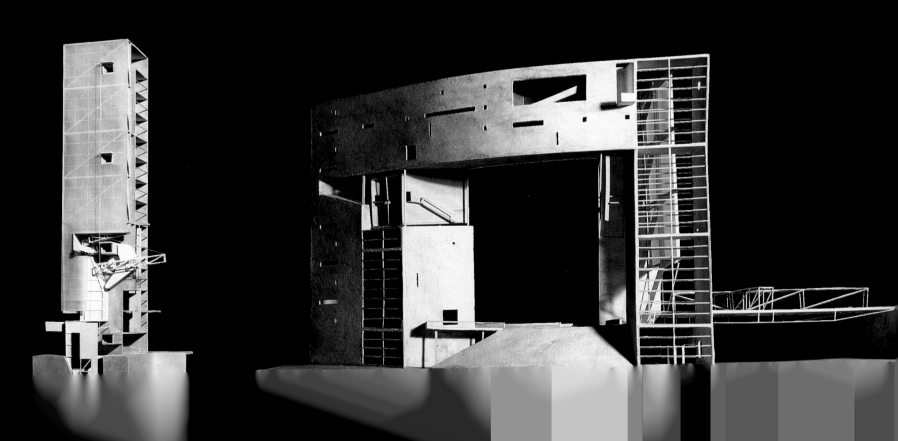

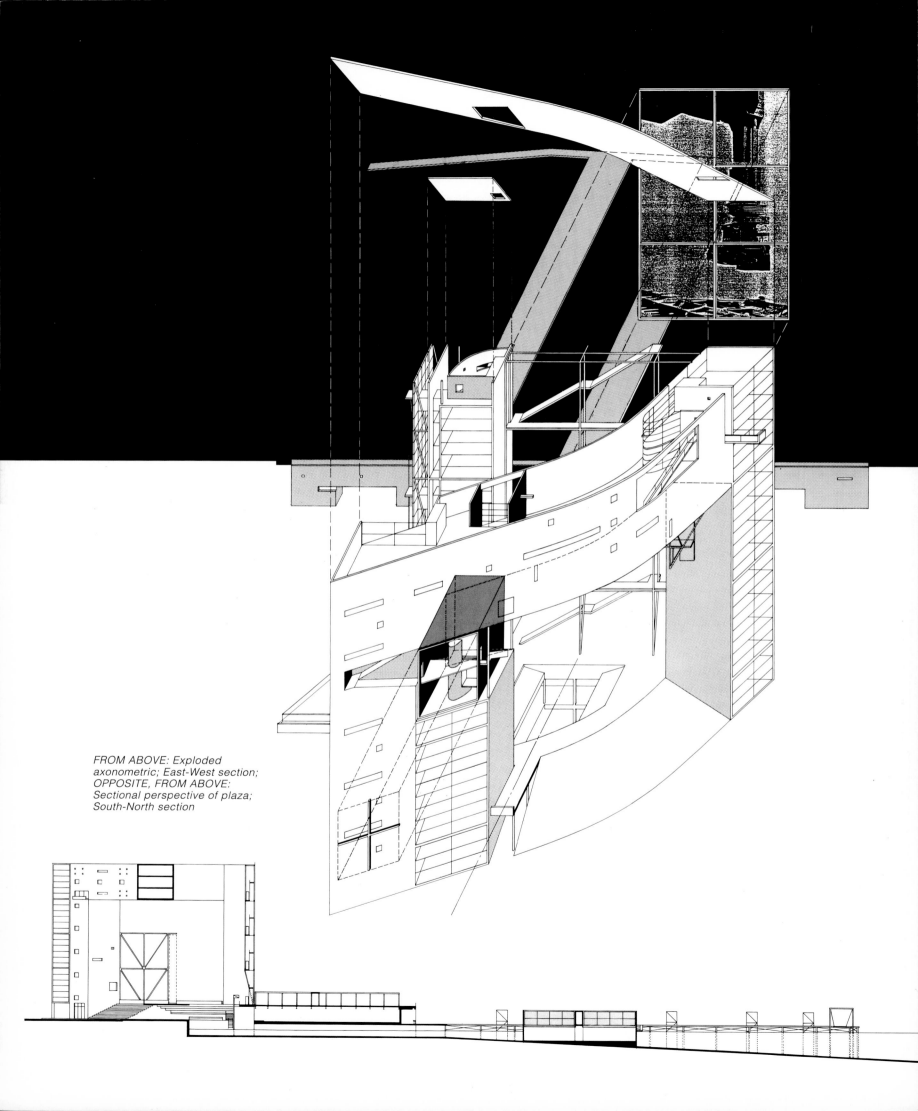

FROM ABOVE: Exploded axonometric; East-West section; OPPOSITE, FROM ABOVE: Sectional perspective of plaza; South-North section

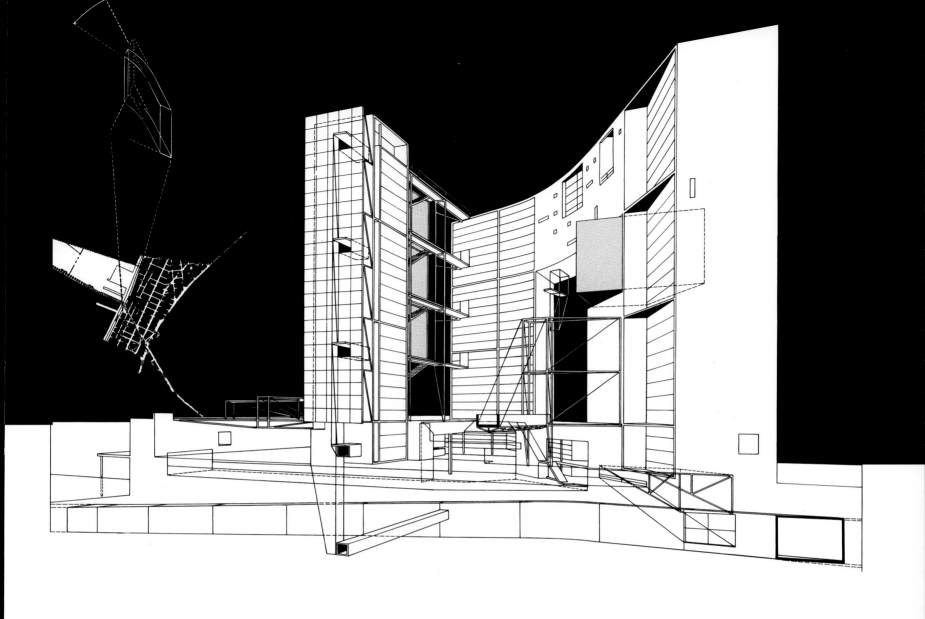

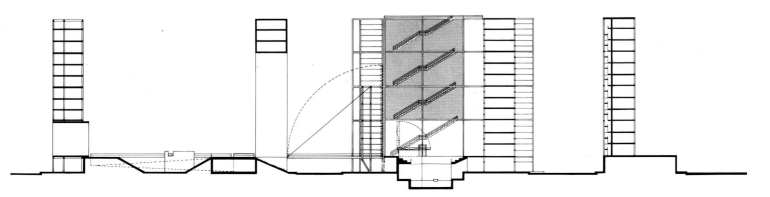

BARTO + BARTO
NANTES REDEVELOPMENT
Nantes, France

Since the 18th century, architects and town planners, like Ceynerey and Crucy, have arranged the sequence, and hierarchy of spaces within the city of Nantes. Their foresight has provided the space allowed for Barto + Barto to explore suitable strategies for living in 1991. The scheme promotes the importance of community life, reconsiders the notions of consumerism and increases the city centre's attraction.

The scheme explores the two themes of water and centrality and is focused on Le Cours des Cinquante Otages, or the place of fifty hostages. This was originally a meander in the local river until it was replaced with a road to ease congestion. Despite being described as the 'lung' of Nantes due to the trees not much space is actually available for pedestrians. This problem is solved by providing space and light for the pedestrians, returning them to the surface, rather than condemning them to underpasses like moles. The importance of the pedestrian and public transport is elevated at the expense of the car. In fact, automobiles are actively slowed down, whilst frequent crossings are provided for the people and priority is given to buses.

Leisure and cultural activities are returned to the centre once more, and Le Cours des Cinquante Otages is reconnected to other nodes within the city, including La Place Feydeau and La Place Alexis Ricordeau. It is, in a way, a redefinition of centrality, with several different centres stretching the heart of the city. A unique and global treatment avoids a hierarchy of functions and produces a city of multiple centres.

The project provides the people of Nantes with space to move, parade and celebrate. Creating an area where crowds can flow where water once did.

OPPOSITE: View of model showing the approach to the plaza; BELOW: View of model, main plaza; OVERLEAF LEFT: View of model, main plaza; PAGE 71: Conceptual explorations

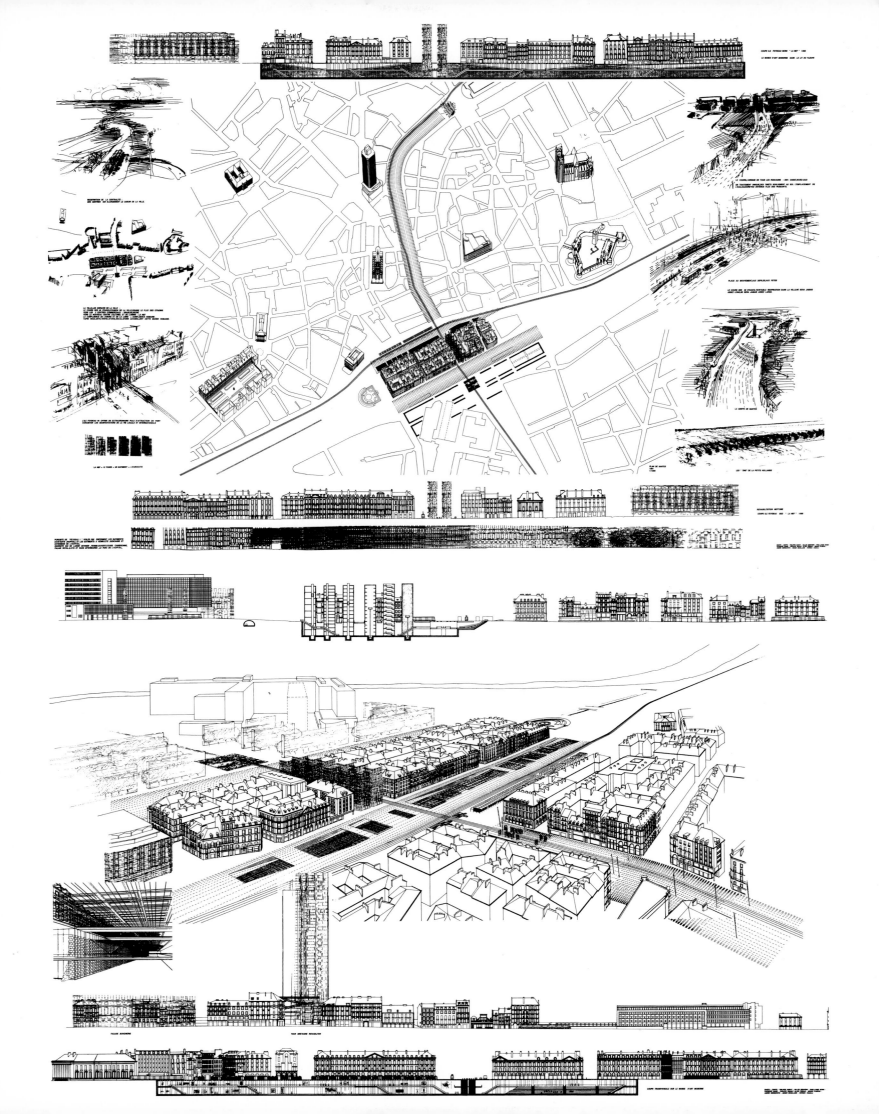

STEVEN EHRLICH

MILLER RESIDENCE
Los Angeles, California

Sunlight and earth, trees and chaparral, animals and birds are the canyon micro-ecology that slices through LA's urban fabric. This residence proclaims the connection with nature by assuming a posture that avoids the obvious canyon vistas, inevitably marred by telephone poles and passing cars. Instead it opts for the more introverted garden and pool. The directness of these connections allows repose and tranquillity.

To cross the threshold from the outside world, into a home, is a cleansing ritual, accompanied by the sound of the water-fall splashing in a slender column over the front door. One enters a central, three-storey, entry atrium that divides the house in two and acts as a light-giving space. Natural light floods in through a skylight, and penetrates the living areas via translucent glass block walls. As if suspended by the light, paths of trans-parent plexiglass, on verendial steel trusses, bridge the atrium, linking the two sides. Shoji screens, in combination with sliding glass that disappears into wall pockets, create a myriad of possibilities in the quality of light, and allow decom-positions in the barrier between indoor and outdoor space.

Rendered perspective

HEMPSTEAD RESIDENCE
Los Angeles

This residence is located in a quiet neighbourhood in the beach community of Venice, California. The client, a television and film director, was interested in a simple, clean space, and found a kindred spirit for the celebration of warm organic colours with her architect. The residence, while rich in colour and vibrancy, is rooted in simple, bold spaces and planes.

As is the tradition in warm weather architecture, the house provides protection from the sun, with recessed doors and windows, and yet spatially connects and fuses internal and external spaces.

The outdoor spaces, at the front and rear, are seamless extensions of the indoor space. The pool and patios are extensions of the living room, whilst the trellised carport doubles as a shaded, covered area, within the arboretum.

The richly coloured stuccos of the exterior, in burnt sienna and yellow ochre, are apparent in the fireplace mantels of the living room and master bedroom; the irregular stone flooring inside and out is from Idaho; the doors and windows are stained fir, and the floors are maple. These organic materials and colours stress that this is a place in harmony with the natural environment.

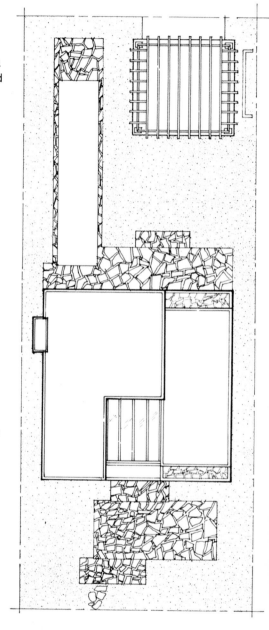

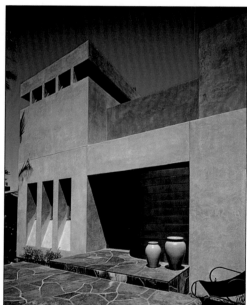

Site plan

74

WINWARD CIRCLE
Los Angeles

Despite being completed in 1991, the Windward Circle is a historical place, a remnant of a bygone dream, a promise for the future. Windward Circle, a roundabout since 1929, was once the lagoon and central convergence system for five principal water canals during Venice's illustrious heyday, fashioned after its eponym in Italy. Venice's current renaissance is now being catalysed, decades after the demolition of these sites, with three new mixed-use projects.

These projects are concerned with creating an urban edge, an animated container for the centre of the circle. The three circle projects resurrect the energy of the past and are, in part, inspired by the reflection in the bygone lagoon of their predecessors.

Spaces will allow flow from the sidewalk on Main Street, and from the rear lot, an agoura-like urban canyon, while two open air stairways draw people to upstairs market areas. The new marketplace is broadcast by a constructivist element at the clipped corner of the building, and instigates the notion of how the original steam driven canal dredger, redefined, becomes a super sign marquee.

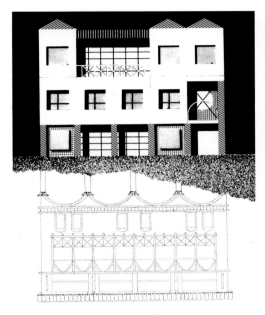

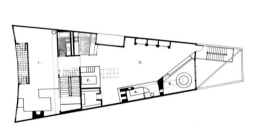

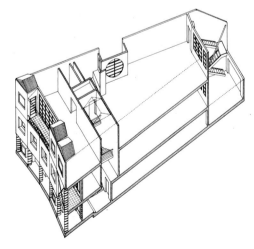

LEFT, FROM ABOVE: Elevation; third floor plan; axonometric

TADAO ANDO

WATER TEMPLE
Honpukuji, Japan

With a revolutionary temple design executed in 1992, Tadao Ando freed Buddhist architecture from some 2,000 years of stylistic shackles (assuming that Chinese palace architecture was more or less fully developed by the Early Han dynasty). To a non-Asian this revolution is perhaps communicated best by the remark of a friend of mine who went temple-hopping in Kyoto recently: 'If you've seen one, you've seen them all.' And he had not even visited China! Buddhism organised in sects cannot claim to have initiated a great variety of architectural form in its long history. On entering the grounds of the Honpukuji temple on Awaji Island, one has to admit that the adjacent traditional buildings have been reduced by Ando's design to embarrassing relics of an unproductive and uncreative past.

Ando did not take up the traditional axial alignment of the main temple buildings and courtyards of the past. Approaching over a vast open area strewn with white pebbles and facing the first very high, bright concrete wall, I was reminded of the crawl-through gate at Fushinan, for here also one is physically made to feel that one is entering. Even though the gate here is more than large enough to pass through in an upright manner, the proportion of the gate to the size of the wall is even smaller than in the case of Fushinan. Where one is entering is not immediately disclosed. Passing over white pebbles along a second, equally high but curved concrete wall, one enters again by suddenly overlooking an oval lotus pond, about forty by thirty metres, bright blue, reflecting the sky. There is no Buddha hall in sight.

The lotus is a venerable symbol in Asia – the channel of origin of all life in Indian cosmogony, and the symbol of self-creation (enlightenment) in Buddhism. A lotus pond spanned by a bridge has long been part of the temple vernacular, but never before have we had to enter the lotus pond in order to recall the temple. Not quite literally, but experientially one enters the pond by descending the staircase in its centre to access the sanctuary.

In contrast to the vastness of the open sky reflected in the pond, the interior of the hall under the convex ceiling (the bottom of the pond) is kept enclosed and dim. Natural light comes through a light room from due west. At sunset, the reddish decor of the sanctuary is brilliantly deepened, heightening the suggestions that one is in the womb.

Honpukuji is affiliated with Shingon, the oldest sect of Tantric Buddhism in Japan, founded in 815 AD. At the core of its training are techniques of meditation using two mandalas, one representing *kongo-kai,* the world of diamond-like transparent wisdom, and the other *taizo-kai,* the 'world of womb-like phenomenal experience'. Two such mandalas hang on either side of the Buddha statue in the Lotus Pond Hall, reminding us that their traditional geometric language is the superimposition of circle and square. Ultimately, their geometry derives from the plans of ancient Indian castles with gates in the four cardinal directions and the monarch placed in the centre surrounded by his army. As the castle expresses worldly power so the mandala came to express spiritual power.

Ando too is playing with those two archetypal shapes or rather he is having us play with them. The circular Buddha hall is opposed to the square reception and tea ceremony rooms laid out with tatami mats and the concrete circular Buddha hall is divided by a square wooden lattice into an outer and an inner realm. Whereas in normal Tantric training one contemplates the two-dimensional surfaces of the two mandalas, Ando immerses the visitor into these two worlds three-dimensionally, forcing us to walk through them and be within them.

Standing out in the open beside the lotus pond above, the interior of the hall is sensed via the long slit-like staircase leading down into it; once inside the red enclosed space of the temple, on the other hand, the vastness of the sky is sensed via the spheroid ceiling. The 'transparent' and womb-like worlds of Shingon are brought into experiential union.

If Ando has anything to teach to Buddhists of this age, then it is by no means the adoption of a new architectural style but rather the truth that the meditative and the intuitive spaces accessible to human experience are the same; they are the source of all creativity, belonging to the *Ursprung.*

Günter Nitschke

OVERLEAF LEFT TO RIGHT: Sections and elevations

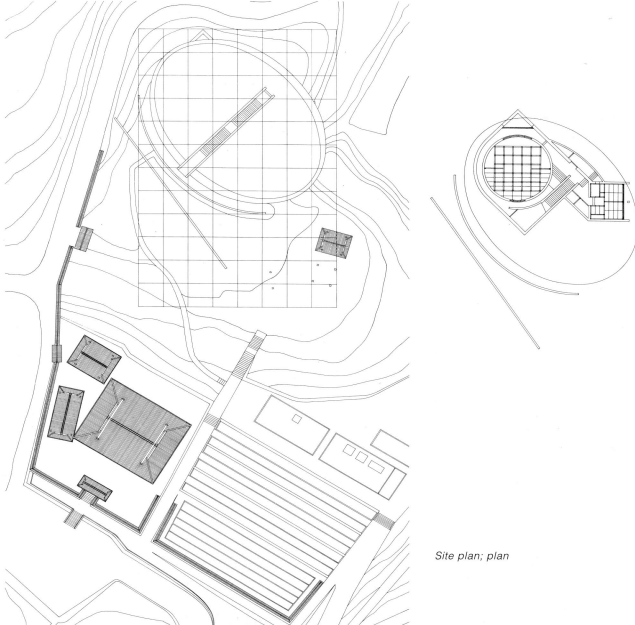

Site plan; plan

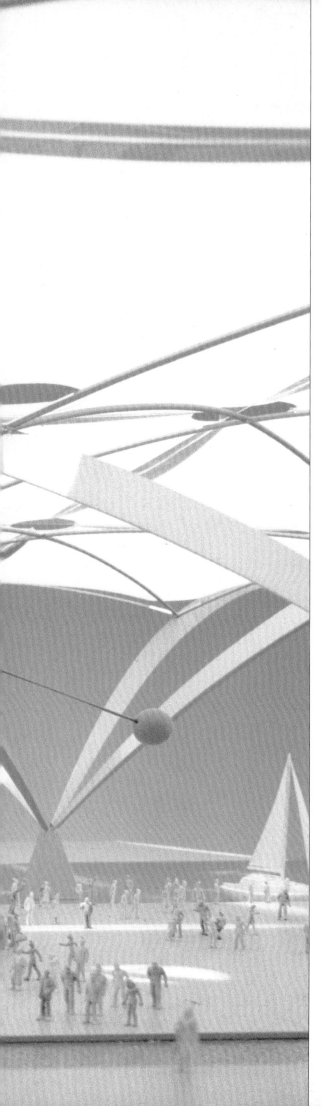

SIR NORMAN FOSTER
EXPOSITION PAVILION
Lisbon, Portugal

The theme for the Lisbon Expo, to be held in 1998, is 'The Ocean's a Heritage for the Future', as the site has a strong association with the sea through its former use as a sea plane dock. Histori-cally, it is claimed that Vasco da Gama set out from here on his voyage to dis-cover the sea route to India. Currently the site is used by the petrochemical industry and for container storage and does not take advantage of the magnificent river frontage. It is very heavily contaminated and a major challenge will be its clean-ing. It has now been announced that Sir Norman Foster and Partners and Sua Kay Architects have won first prize, along with four other Portuguese architects, in an open ideas competition on how the site should be developed.

In total the site is five kilometres long and approximately 310 hectares. Within this is a notional 25 hectares that is the site for the Exposition. The site is also to contain Lisbon's new high speed rail station, 80 hectares of housing and additional office and industrial space. There will be pavilions for national dis-plays, for companies, the oceans, arts centre, as well as a multipurpose, Uto-pian, and communications.

Many of the recent Expos are a sprawl of individual buildings, each vying for attention. Like the suburbs, the typical Expo has no centre, no heart, no sense of place. When the visitors leave, the life of the Expo is over and leaves dead spaces. All that investment, expense and effort is wasted on an event that lasts only three months. The experience of the last century, particularly that of the 1851 Great Exhibition at Crystal Palace, suggests that consolidating the exhibition is a more successful approach. Instead of an international free-for-all, Expo 98 should be a statement about Lisbon and Portugal. It should, like a small town, be built for the future, rather than just the Expo's duration; a long, instead of short, term investment.

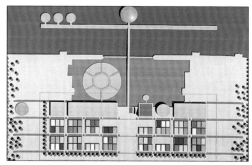

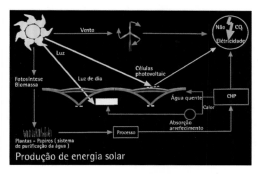

Produção de energia solar

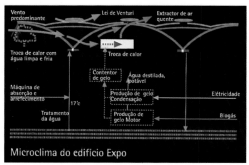

Microclima do edifício Expo

OPPOSITE: Model of Exhibition Hall interior; FROM ABOVE: Site plan of Exhibition Hall; Aerial photomontage of site; computer generated explanation of microclimate within Exhibition Hall; computer generated explana-tion of solar behaviour within Exhibition Hall; OVERLEAF, FROM ABOVE L TO R: Model of site; model of Exhibition Hall exterior; model of Exhibition Hall interior

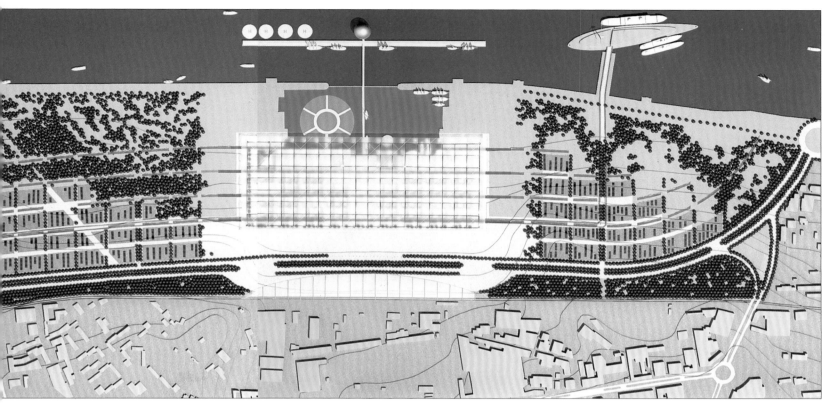

BARCELONA MASTERPLAN
Spain

Throughout its two thousand year history, Barcelona has been an international city. Its strategic location on the Mediterranean Sea served as a principal European port with reaches as far as Africa and the Orient. Its proximity to France gave northern Europe entry to the Iberian Peninsula and beyond. In conjunction with its role as host of the 1992 Summer Olympic Games, Barcelona has undertaken massive urban renewal, with projects ranging from the redesign of its infrastructure to the creation of parks and public spaces. The imminent arrival of the TGV and the country's growing position within the European Community reinforces the city's international standing.

Barcelona is now a city with enormous potential and fantastic opportunities for the future. It is in this context and with this spirit of enthusiasm that the Sagrera Station project has been approached. The possibility for growth within the city must be carefully managed, and greatest use must be made of existing land and assets if Barcelona is not to proliferate as an urban sprawl. The 230 hectares of underused railway and industrial lands, identified as the Sagrera site, is a golden opportunity for the city to plan now for its growth in the next millennium. The project team proposes an integrated and comprehensive masterplan which will enable maximum advantage to be achieved by the city from this bold scheme.

The proposed masterplan creates a striking, but simple, framework in which the necessary homes, jobs and cultural activities, the city requires, can be created. Focused on a new six kilometre-long park and water course, the plan works with the existing elements of the city on its edges, and links them together to form a new piece of urban fabric. The Sagrera Station site amounts to approximately three per cent of the land area within Barcelona's new inner beltway. As a relatively thin, but long, area of rail and industrial land, it stretches from Placa de les Glories to the city's north east and the new beltway interchange at Trinitat.

This new city, within the existing city, maintains the richness of activity that Barcelona generates through its mixed use buildings. Whilst the development will create a new commercial centre for Barcelona, it will be fully integrated with new infrastructure; extensive underground parking, homes, retail, and cultural facilities. All of the existing communities, and the new one that will grow with them, will have direct access to the new park.

All of these new opportunities will be created through maximising the advantages the TGV offers by creating a new station as the development's focus. In seizing this opportunity now, and by rationalising and minimising the impact of running tracks, this area will be reborn.

OPPOSITE: Detail of model showing water and landscaping; FROM ABOVE: CAD view across masterplan showing lake through the middle; detail of masterplan model

RICHARD ROGERS
NEW COMMUNITY MASTERPLAN
Balearic Islands

Introduction

The Government of the Balearic Islands became interested in developing a pilot urban project which would create a community in which key professionals could live and work. The hope was to attract funding from the EC and raise the professional base of the Balearic Islands.

The competition, held in May 1994, called for ideas for an urban development which made maximum use of the islands' natural resources. Ten international teams were invited, including Sir Norman Foster & Partners, Hisho Hara and Koetter Kim, and also Spanish and local teams. In the competition the Partnership won the highest number of awards, and were particularly strong in the category concerned with landscape and ecology.

The site is approximately two kilometres square, and is eight kilometres north of Palma at the base of the mountains. The climatic conditions prevalent on the island result in arid summers, when water is scarce, and very wet winters. The brief required a residential population of 3,000 people and, a peak working population of some 7-8,000 people.

Urban Concept

The aim was to create a vibrant publicly focused community within an enriched rural landscape, which would make best use of the naturally available resources on the site. The plan was assembled by analysis of the following elements with the intention of creating an integrated and efficient community:

Social Fabric: The urban community is made up of three villages. Public activities are concentrated at the centre of each cluster and diffuse out to quieter residential areas on the periphery.

Water: Rainfall is collected in the winter storms and is used to irrigate crops throughout the summer

Agriculture: The scheme aims to diversify the existing crops from olive trees and carobs, to include potatoes, onions and strawberries.

Transport: The proposals focus on a hierarchical transportation system, emphasising public rather that the private transport, which includes a tram system.

Energy: The irrigation system allows high energy crops to be grown, which are gasified providing local power.

Use of Water as an Amenity

The winter storm waters run through the site along two small valleys, separated by a spur of land. They are collected into two new lakes that form the focus for two of the three villages. The third village, which is more business oriented, sits on the central spur enjoying excellent views over the site.

The lakes are full in the winter and the level of water falls gradually over the summer as water is taken for irrigation and drinking. As the level of the water falls, so the shore of the lake steps down to expose walkways and spaces for sitting alongside the shore. Devices, that capture the sun's energy are revealed to provide shade and power small water pumps to aerate the water, thus controlling the spread of mosquitoes.

Use of Water for Irrigation

The water is distributed by a series of channels in the upper reaches of the site, and by gravity lower down to irrigate a series of agricultural terraces, or soil sinks. The soil in these terraces contains a high level of organic matter that retains water increasing the moisture content. Crops that require more moisture, such as onions, strawberries and tomatoes, are grown in the wetter upper terraces. Lower demand crops such as potatoes and maize are grown in the lower terraces.

On the lower and flatter areas of the site simple underground pipes irrigate the fields enhancing productivity. The intent is to grow energy crops, such as sweet sorghum and willow, in these areas. These crops grow quickly and are coppiced over a period of years and then used as fuel to power small local generation stations. This method of generating power means that CO_2 levels in the environment are not increased and as the power is close to urban developments and waste can be used for heating housing and schools.

Neighbourhood

The central lakes are a vital part of the urban infrastructure as well as being a social amenity. They provide a cool central focus to the dense pockets of urban activity in the centre of each cluster rather than a congested, and polluted, town centre.

Integrated Approach

Overall, a wide range of urban issues and problems were examined from early on in the design process. Engineering and specialist expertise were integrated into the project from the start to ensure that the development worked with the island rather than against it.

OPPOSITE, FROM ABOVE: Model of earth sheltered housing; model of public buildings around the lake

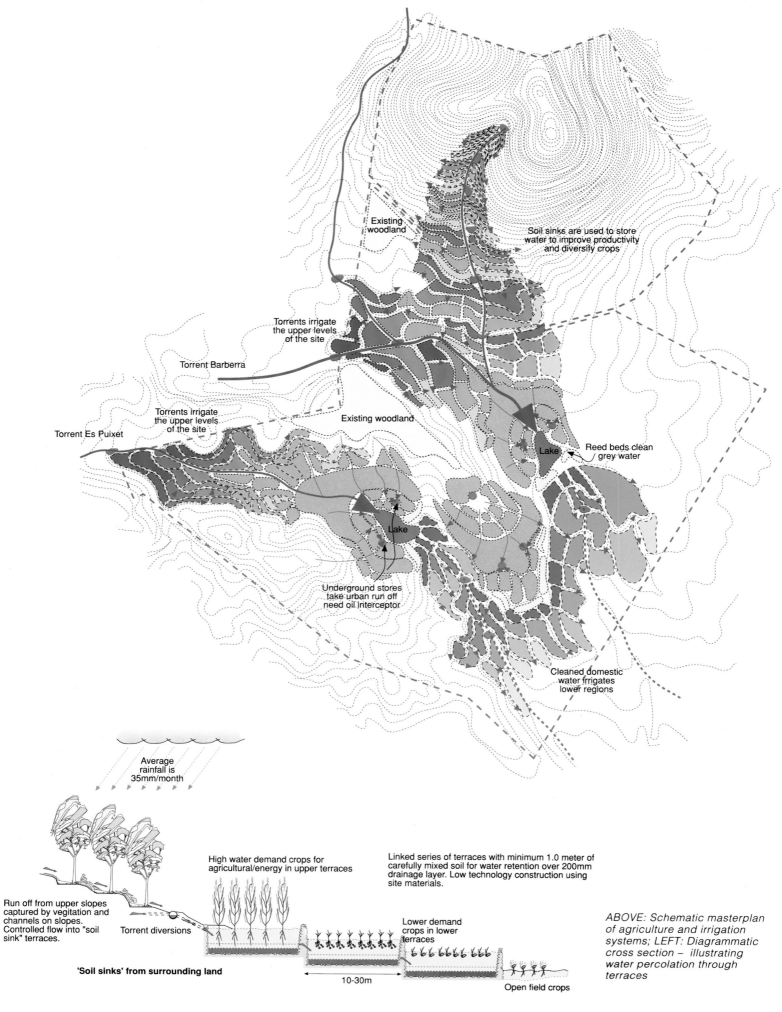

Existing
woodland

Soil sinks are used to store
water to improve productivity
and diversify crops

Torrents irrigate
the upper levels
of the site

Torrent Barberra

Torrents irrigate
the upper levels
of the site

Existing woodland

Torrent Es Puixet

Lake

Reed beds clean
grey water

Lake

Underground stores
take urban run off
need oil interceptor

Cleaned domestic
water irrigates
lower regions

Average
rainfall is
35mm/month

High water demand crops for
agricultural/energy in upper terraces

Linked series of terraces with minimum 1.0 meter of
carefully mixed soil for water retention over 200mm
drainage layer. Low technology construction using
site materials.

Run off from upper slopes
captured by vegitation and
channels on slopes.
Controlled flow into "soil
sink" terraces.

Torrent diversions

Lower demand
crops in lower
terraces

'Soil sinks' from surrounding land

10-30m

Open field crops

*ABOVE: Schematic masterplan
of agriculture and irrigation
systems; LEFT: Diagrammatic
cross section – illustrating
water percolation through
terraces*

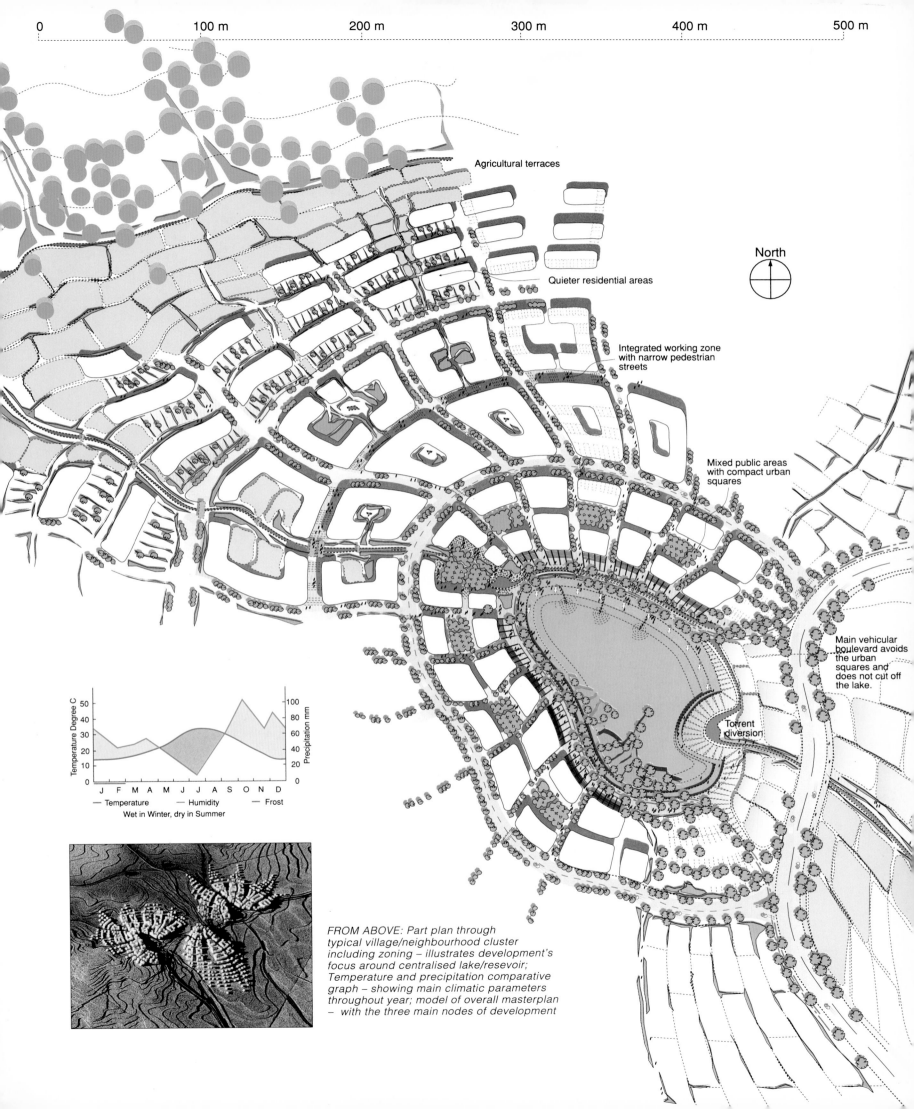

0   100 m   200 m   300 m   400 m   500 m

Agricultural terraces

Quieter residential areas

North

Integrated working zone with narrow pedestrian streets

Mixed public areas with compact urban squares

Main vehicular boulevard avoids the urban squares and does not cut off the lake.

Torrent diversion

Temperature Degree C
Precipitation mm
50
40
30
20
10
0
J F M A M J J A S O N D
— Temperature   — Humidity   — Frost
Wet in Winter, dry in Summer
100
80
60
40
20
0

FROM ABOVE: Part plan through typical village/neighbourhood cluster including zoning – illustrates development's focus around centralised lake/resevoir; Temperature and precipitation comparative graph – showing main climatic parameters throughout year; model of overall masterplan – with the three main nodes of development

PUMP HOUSE
Royal Victoria Dock, London

The scheme provides a water pumping station at the confluence of new, deep underground channels, to lift waste water up to a high level for discharge into the River Thames. It is a key part of the new infrastructure for the Royal Docks that will enable a proper urban environment to be created in the area.

The site is particularly prominent being situated at the principal entrance to the docks and so the pump house naturally becomes a strong visual landmark and 'gateway' building. The predominant design necessity was to organise the servicing and operational requirements above ground level into a long life, low maintenance, rugged building that would integrate its engineering function and its architecture into a clear, simple and visually exuberant expression of the working operation.

The solution consists of two concentric drums, rising 12 metres above ground level. Their inner, 25 metre-deep, shafts, and attendant screens, pumps and pipe risers, are placed axially in the direction of the water flow, which is itself regulated by radially housed electrical support equipment. All heavy submersible pumps and equipment can be reached by annular crane ways housed in the main pump hall.

Concrete surfaces are brightly coloured, whilst steelwork and services are boldly detailed to overcome the remote and unfriendly characteristics commonly found in municipal uninhabited buildings of this type. Lightweight curtain walls, that need to be highly damage-resistant, but nevertheless translucent, are made of white polycarbonate sheet set in a steel frame that provides an interesting contrast to the surrounding materials. Overall, Rogers has used bold colours and detailing to articulate a building which otherwise would have been considered an eyesore.

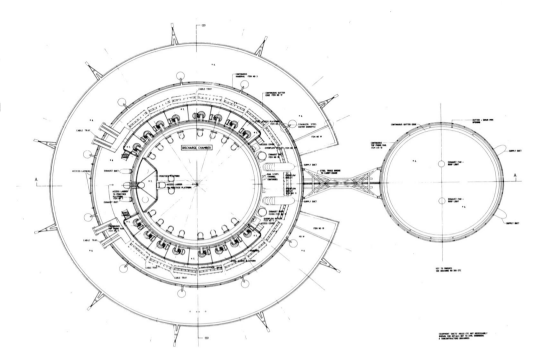

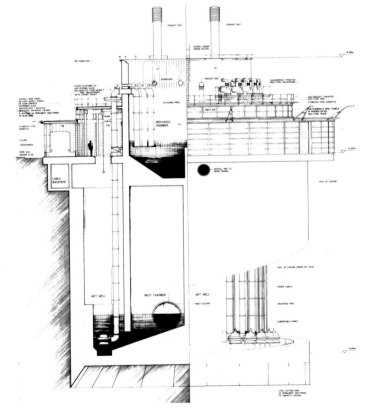

FROM ABOVE: Roof level plan; cross section

WILLIAM PYE
THE APPEAL OF WATER

Water is a seductive element, and its beguiling qualities appeal to our most basic instincts. If one considers the mass appeal of the Trevi fountain, or those in the Piazza Navona, a synthesis of sculpture and water is apparent. The presence of water has helped the sculptures to become so universally appreciated: people are drawn to fountains, waterfalls and water features in a way that is often denied to other public sculptures.

It is those repetitive, yet infinitely complex and ever changing patterns of water which are so mesmeric and compulsive; something akin to the hypnotic effect of staring into a flickering fire, each lick of flame repeating itself, yet different every time.

 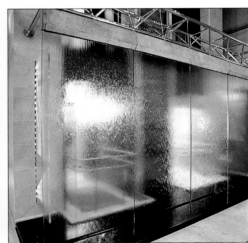

OPPOSITE: Cristos, St Christopher's Place, London; FROM ABOVE L TO R: Ebbw Font, Ebbw Vale, Wales; Epidavros, Dolby Laboratories, Wootton Bassett, Wiltshire; Arethusa, Unicorn House, London; Chalice, Fountain Square, London; Aventino, Mercury House, London; Aventino, Mercury House, London (pictured OVERLEAF)